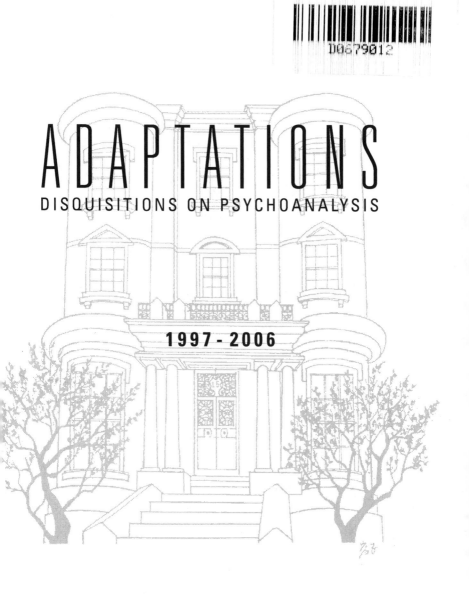

ADAPTATIONS
DISQUISITIONS ON PSYCHOANALYSIS

1997 - 2006

Printed in the United States of America.

ISBN 10: 1-59571-216-X
ISBN 13: 978-1-59571-216-5

Library of Congress Control Number: 2007937595

Publishers

Hanns Sachs Library and Archives
of the Boston Psychoanalytic Society
and Institute, Inc.

Word Association Publishers
205 Fifth Avenue
Tarentum, Pennsylvania 15084

www.wordassociation.com
1.800.827.7903

Book design: Gina Datres, Word Association Publishers
Paintings and line art: Jonathan Palmer

ADAPTATIONS

DISQUISITIONS ON PSYCHOANALYSIS

1997 - 2006

PHILLIP FREEMAN, M.D.

A PUBLICATION OF THE
HANNS SACHS LIBRARY AND ARCHIVES
OF THE BOSTON PSYCHOANALYTIC SOCIETY
AND INSTITUTE, INC.

Boston, Massachusetts

THIS BOOK IS DEDICATED TO
EDWARD M. WEINSHEL, M.D.

CONTENTS

FOREWORD
By Alan Pollock, M.D.

"I suppose we should start with the pigs" (2003). Or should we begin with the turtles? The jellyfish? The nuns, alchemists, or tarantists? Perhaps we should give pride of place to The Greats and begin with Hans Holbein the Younger or Erasmus, Shakespeare, or even Freud. Or maybe fabulists like the Trappist-herpetologist-poikilotherapist-psychoanalyst Guy Pinterra (1999). And surely we must take note of the entire collection of personages from the Boston Psychoanalytic Society and Institute, about and for whom these glorious diversions are composed.

Through Phillip Freeman's wondrously deft and daft disquisitions, all these worthies and a host of others dance an intricate and exuberant tarantella. As they swirl around us, braiding a pattern that we almost but never for long grasp clearly, they wink and tease and, repeatedly, surprise. The most improbable partners join hands, and we laugh at the unimagined rightness of such incongruities. A pig or turtle or poikilotherapist catches our eye, then disappears into the whirling throng, lost to sight and nearly forgotten as his place is instantly filled by a nun or alchemist or analyst. Then comes the startling instant when the nearly forgotten pig or turtle or poikilotherapist flashes back into sight, and we see how his steps mimic and reflect and comment on those of the nun or alchemist or analyst. Ceaseless kaleidoscopic delights.

Perhaps every subject matter begets its own truest form of humor. Phillip Freeman's monologues are that for psychoanalysis. In form, could we imagine more distilled free associations? Seemingly random juxtapositions, preposterous propinquities, turn out to be structured implicitly to triangulate and illuminate pervasive themes of unrest in contemporary psychoanalysis. The arcane scholarship; the fascination with history, ancestors, and death; the stretch for scientific grounding—many of the preoccupations of psychoanalytic writing are mirrored and parodied in these monologues. And of course, to help us bear distress is the common task of both psychoanalysis and humor: "Humor is the instinct for taking pain playfully" (Max Eastman).

Distress? Our field is lively these days, and our practices are more robust than seemed likely a decade ago. Yet "we have reason to suspect the presence of Dark Forces" (2005).

We fear that we dance our tarantella on quicksand. Even Phillip's reminder that "there are reasons to be optimistic . . . about quicksand" (2006) doesn't quite relieve the anxiety. Here, in paraphrase, is how Phillip describes the subject of his discourse:

We are a profession trying to hold onto its dignity and our identity during a time of attack. Market forces press us to dumb down truth. Can we hold onto what's important while adapting through outreach, greater inclusiveness, and assimilation of challenges posed by empirical science?

"Bad humor is an evasion of reality; good humor is an acceptance of it" (Malcolm Muggeridge). The reality that Phillip addresses is the same one lamented by Susan Sontag: "Almost everything in our debauched culture invites us to simplify reality, to despise wisdom." In such a culture, psychoanalysis flounders. Phillip's masterful presentations play with the pain of our dilemma as they chronicle our flailings of avoidance and silliness.

Phillip created and performed the monologues in this book as entertainments for the annual graduation dinner party of the Boston Psychoanalytic Society and Institute, 1997-2006. Imagine the plight of the rest of us on the program, approaching our mundane duties—acknowledging graduates or thanking staff and faculty or exhorting the membership—armed against the potential humiliations of public speaking with no more than the typical after-dinner speaker's joke or anecdote. No one wants to follow Phillip on the dais. No one wants even to speak on the same program as Phillip. Maybe not speak again ever ... anywhere.

We are dwarfed not only by the brilliance of Phillip's writing, but by the theater of his presentation, the uniquely matter-of-fact timbre and pace of his voice as he glides among his sparkling non sequiturs as if nothing more remarkable were happening than the recitation of yet another ordinary academic paper. I recommend that you read each of these monologues straight through, letting it flow past even if you are confused by the kaleidoscope of images and ideas. The pattern emerges from the whole, a woven gestalt. Then, if you are intrigued, go back to catch the individual threads.

Fortunately at least some of the monologues have been recorded, and four are being made available on a CD accompanying this volume. Three of them (1997, 1998, 2004) are live recordings. The laughs are real. The 2006 recording was made for this CD, without an audience.

Enjoy.

PREFACE

One hand on the gunnel,
What shall we bring?
Where shall we go?

Tsol Yenom, "Crested Not Benthic"

Freud famously loved gallows humor. It is the moment, if only a moment, in which wit defies harsh reality. Psychoanalysts rally to the cause of defiant wit. There is much to defy. The pendulum swings from the individual to the group, from the solo practitioner to the corporation, from the guild member to the employee. Professions fade away, and their oaths and codes are replaced by contracts and regulations. The marketplace and the Zeitgeist conspire to subvert the time and nuance required for attention to the individual life and psyche. Even so, we psychoanalysts struggle to hold onto the fragile and distinctive concepts and techniques that offer hope and meaning to our patients and ourselves.

And yet. Our efforts to hold onto our dignity sometimes fall short. Badly. Our efforts to adapt, to market ourselves, to reach out, to self-promote sometimes do not show our field at its best. Our efforts to integrate with the academy, medicine, science, and the community sometimes fail to demonstrate our grasp of the limits of our technique, our world, and ourselves. Still. What else can we do?

Fortunately for me and, probably, for the field, psychoanalysts, and those who bear with them, love to laugh. They laugh at the world, at each other, and at themselves. Also fortunate for me is the fact that psychoanalysts, accustomed as they are to listening for the representation

of complex themes in displacement and in inexact autobiography, typically hang in there and wait for sense to appear. It is a quality that
makes for a good and generous audience.

Regarding the names of individuals and professional associations: For
those outside of or unfamiliar with Boston psychoanalytic organizations, the Boston Psychoanalytic Society and Institute goes by the
acronym BPSI, pronounced "bip-see." The Psychoanalytic Institute of
New England, PINE, is also cited. Other named individuals include
Diana Nugent, the administrative director of BPSI, and some of the
presidents of the Boston Psychoanalytic Society—Gerry Adler, Jackie
Zilbach, Jeff Nason, and Len Glass—whose tenure occurred during the
ten-year stretch covered by these talks. Other villagers, including mem-
bers and members-in-training at BPSI, and members of the American
Psychoanalytic Association, should be recognizable as such in context.
Certain individuals, including professors Zahi Hawass and Chikaosa
Tanimoto, appear in imagined settings and interactions.

Regarding the enclosed CD: The talks were recorded at the Wellesley
College Faculty Club on the occasion of the annual gathering of the
BPSI community. The recording equipment was somewhat less than
modest. Each talk was delivered once, from memory. Four of the ten
recorded talks are included—warts, neologisms, dropped phrases and
all—on the CD. Ideally, they capture, at the least, evidence of the
warmth of the occasions and the great generosity of the audience.

ACKNOWLEDGMENTS

I would like to thank Tony Kris, whose boundless energy, initiative, and leadership during the most trying of times keeps us afloat. He instigated this publication, gathered the many colleagues whose generous support made this publication possible, and, not for the first time, pointed me toward the finish line. I am indebted to the membership of the Boston Psychoanalytic Society and Institute, the largest such institution in the United States. Their many activities are a testimony to the vitality of psychoanalytic research, training, and practice. They comprise a congregation full of the love and the fight that bespeaks a passionate commitment to the profession. Peter Wohlauer, in particular, provides the words and the example that help me to keep the faith. Jonathan Palmer generously contributed his artwork for the book jacket and illustrations. Diana Nugent and the BPSI administrative staff have been supportive and helpful. Nancy Moore Hulnick contributed invaluable and expert editorial assistance. Dan Flynn used his considerable expertise to produce the CD. Gina Datres (Word Association Publishers) contributed her personal warmth and unerring eye for design. Finally, I would like to thank my wife and children. They make allowances. They make contributions. They make it all worthwhile.

BPSI 1997
OUTREACH: GERRY

Let's say you are one of Susumu Tonegawa's mice . . .

You think you're fine, you grow up fine, but it turns out that a particular gene was knocked out of your embryonic stem cells when you were a blastocyst, so now your hippocampus is missing a part so when you go swimming with your friends in a bath of water dyed milky white with tempera they can find their way back to a submerged platform but you can't find your way home. Don't you think that would be disturbing? Don't you think that would be a little disorienting?

So, I'm driving through Central Square with Diana Nugent and Gerry Adler to get the dirt for our front yard because the facade of psychoanalysis poisoned the soil and nothing will grow there anymore and Gerry is quoting Isaiah about foundations. And I think of the Danish neuroscientist on the airplane to London who asked me—I was a college sophomore at the time—about my interests, and when I got to psychoanalysis he said, "Then you should become a rabbi." So when I saw my rabbi I said I was interested in psychoanalysis and he said, "*My* son will be a developer of real estate."

So Jackie Zilbach reported, after the storm, that our gardening consultant had pronounced the magnolias dead and said that our facade had poisoned the soil so that nothing would grow there anymore. Please understand that this is literally true, however suggestive: when the face of the institute, the face of psychoanalysis in Boston, was washed a few years back it created a precipitant that bled into the soil, a precipitant so toxic that nothing will grow in our garden ever again. So, when Jackie hit us up on the spot for cash so that you would all follow our example and Diana looked at the checks that we passed to the end of the table and recorded the amounts in her ledger book, it was just like Rabbi Katz (before he had us removed for waving our noise-makers when he mentioned Esther instead of when he mentioned Haman) used to say: "We've received a donation of $100 to the floral fund from Jack and Florence Siegel in honor of the bat mitzvah of their daughter Ruth."

So I called him, the rabbi. He said his son was putting up condos in Cambridge and had the dirt. Gerry said he knew the spot. He wanted to drive. Diana gave me a look because we knew that since the foundation came up, Gerry's been different. He gets excited. He forgets things. Gerry calls me at night. He says, "Did you hear it? Did you hear Clinton quote Isaiah on foundations during the inaugural?" I said that I had. Gerry shouts, "Behold I lay in Zion for a *foundation* a *stone*." I answer, "A *tried* stone, a *precious* stone, a *sure foundation!*"

I shouldn't have encouraged him. During the leadership retreat for the Executive Council that Tsol Yenom set up at the Kabuki baths downtown, Gerry was paddling about the tempera bath trying to find his way back to the checkered tile bench under the white water when he had an epiphany.

He said, "I can't be a one-note piano."

"You're not," I told him. It was ten thirty at night and *Chicago Hope* was on.

He said, "The foundation has to belong to everyone."

"It will, Gerry."

This was the *Chicago Hope* where they introduce the psychiatrist. The one who plays a nylon-stringed guitar and sings, "You've got to have high hopes ... " to his patients. The one who looks exactly like

Mandel Fogel, my old boss at the surgical supply house who, one day, after two years of my working stock, allowed me to deliver a hospital bed to Mrs. Iskols at 44 Cedar Street in some Long Island town where I got lost inside my first poem.

You have to understand a difference between Boston and Long Island. In Boston the signs, the signage, indicate where you can go but not where you are. The signs are about future possibilities. Very forward-looking. On Long Island, at the intersections of all public thoroughfares, there are sets of signs that allow you to exactly identify your position. You are locked in the present, but it is a discontinuous present because the name of the street on which you are driving seems to randomly appear, disappear, and reappear in new locations or altered forms as you cross the unmarked boundaries along an endless stream of commuter towns. And so, somewhere down the line of lost and found Cedar Streets in Valley Stream Lynbrook Rockville Center Baldwin Freeport Merrick Bellmore Massapequa Massapequa Park Amityville Copague Lindenhurst and Babylon, I was delayed. And Mandel Fogel, my boss, a lieutenant in the auxiliary police force, told officers of the peace that I had stolen his truck.

Diana seems to be considering a similar course of action as Gerry peers over the steering wheel. He looks concerned. Gerry is having an *unheimlich* experience. He's sure he's at the right construction site, but the buildings around it look strange and unfamiliar. We get out and start filling the wheelbarrow with loam. Diana's getting cranky. She had not realized that we would *literally* be shoveling the dirt. She starts questioning Gerry's assumptions about the site, and Gerry, who knows that objective authority is an illusion, tells Diana that her remark has led him to associate to his experience of being forced onto the birthing mat during our recent jointly sponsored Therapeutic Modalities Conference.

Now, I don't have a corner on the truth, but this memory is a distortion. Gerry was, in fact, a birthing mat *enthusiast*. On the occasion of his delivery, several of us lined up on each side of this mat—it must have been twenty feet long—and Gerry began this backward crab walk down the canal and we're pushing and shoving and Pat Wright's manipulating the breech and Martha Stark is doing the cord around the neck and Gerry finishes, looking flushed and, I think, understandably disoriented. He says he's fine.

No one is uncomfortable with disorientation anymore. The candidates I've had the pleasure to know in recent years are as happily uncertain as pigs in milk baths. They love the dark. They were raised in the Night Kitchen. Tsol, our former financial, sometime theory, consultant, now our gardening consultant, tells me it's the Zeitgeist. He's back from his Albania experiment. He says that the riots and the characterization of his program as a golden pyramid scheme were press distortions. He says he was simply applying the principles of health care delivery on a larger scale in a smaller place. "There was nothing revolutionary," he says modestly. "The revolution, the *paradigm shift*, occurred twenty-five years ago when we learned that you could make a profit by selling corporations a way to not provide health care benefits and to collect a fee proportional to the nonprovision of services. That was genius. The rest is details." In Albania, Tsol provided the ministers with a plan in which they promised absolutely everything, collected all the money from a destitute populace, and provided absolutely nothing.

He got away uninjured. He blamed the disturbances on a failure of support staff. He made it back to D.C. to report on Albania to a health policy think tank of Fortune 500 CEOs, modestly called the Round

Table, but now he's discouraged. "These *machers*, it's always the same. They only care about one goddamn thing: *psychoanalytic theory*. And they're so P.C.! Every man/woman among them is an Authentic, Spontaneous, Self-Disclosing, Empath ... Paternalistic this and Contextualized that ... Constructivists and Interpersonalists ... And everything the analyst says is said out of ignorance or arrogance or self-deception, and if the patient seems better it's only because the analyst was finally able to tolerate what the patient was trying to say all along. Yadda yadda. In my home, when the Object of the Other returned, He knew how to lay down the Law of Laws!"

So Tsol is taking a sabbatical as our financial/theory consultant. He's tending the nursery.

I tell him it's the same in Boston. We've been cleaning our theoretical house. Only the unconscious is left, and even that Maginot Line was crossed a few months ago when Owen Renik came to town and filled our theater like Woodstock, people spilling down the hallways into the street, and George Fishman gets up to announce, "You people are *incredible!* You've shut down Storrow *Drive*, Man!" I sat on the floor at Ed Shapiro's feet, enormous feet, a position I'd struggled to avoid for three years at McLean, just to hear Owen pronounce the unconscious dead—no more dusty bins of yesterday's memories—he prefers an unconscious that has not happened yet. A co-constructed unconscious full of meanings and possibilities. Very forward-looking. I say to the candidates, "Doesn't it ever *bother* you?" and one of them tells me, with what sounds suspiciously like *authority*, that I am suffering the Terror of Intersubjectivity. So I tell Diana, "Diana, you are suffering the Terror of Intersubjectivity." She wipes her brow, puts down her shovel, and pushes me into the hole.

———

Joan Wheelis is graduating tonight. No Terror of Intersubjectivity there. Ten years ago we were out paddling in a Puget Sound sea of bioluminescent plankton near her family compound and I pointed out to her that our paddle had just disappeared beneath the glow and she said, "Ten years from tonight I will graduate from the Boston Psychoanalytic Institute. I expect you to be there and to be wearing an aubergine suit." Some people know how to plan. Some people know just where they are in the Scheme of Things.

Tsol has the front yard patch covered with a white gauze. There's no evidence of growth, but rain puddles on the gauze have attracted mice and the neighbors are starting to complain. "Let them complain! My flock has found its way home to the undergarden!" We ask Tsol his plans for the garden. "Well, I tell you it's been a process. First I was thinking Zen, reflective. Cool but hard. Very one-person psychology. So then I thought Formal French. Academic sheen. Babes. But an institute cannot live by groupies alone. So then I thought faux natural British, inviting greenery, little Maresfield Gardens, totem and taboo antiquities for garden sculpture. But it's nostalgic. Get over yourself, Tsol. So then I was thinking about Robert Smithson, the earthworks sculptor who built a football field–sized stone boulder jetty out into the Great Salt Lake. He knew that before it was even finished the rising water level and the salt crystals would submerge the whole works so that, a few years later, no one could even tell where it had been. Smithson understood the process. So I began to think about the undergarden. The unseen spring."

Tsol pauses to watch Gerry lurching about the median strip of Commonwealth Avenue in his sackcloth, carrying the hoe over his shoulder. Gerry's taken to calling himself The Caretaker. He's shouting up at the people in the brownstones, "Come out! Come out and take your medicine!"

I tell Tsol about Gerry and Isaiah. Tsol says, "Isaiah helped a weak king and a frightened people through uncertain times. The Lord had planted a vineyard with his choicest vines but then he laid it waste. Hezekiah ignored Isaiah's advice, made a devil's bargain with the Egyptians, and got overridden with Assyrians. The people, looking for shortcuts, fell back on oblations and ritual sacrifice. But Isaiah believed that a remnant, a 'Sacred Remnant,' would remember the Covenant and that Israel would 'blossom and bud and fill the face of the world with fruit' again."

By this point, the mice were gathered unnaturally around Tsol's feet. He raised his arms. "*Boray p'ree hagoffen*, little fellas. May the face of our institute blossom and bud and fill with fruit." And then, this to me: "But, until that day comes, don't forget the floral fund."

BPSI 1998
ADAPTATION: THE SPHINX

As of this year the average age of the American Psychoanalytic Association membership has reached the eighth and final Eriksonian stage of life. At the December meeting of the membership committee, Zahi Hawass, chief inspector of antiquities for Egypt's Giza Plateau, represented the organization's age demographics as an inverted pyramid; the same inverted pyramid, he told us, that had been used by pharaohs since the time of the Otukungurua to depict the decision of a people to end their line through an act of communal infertility in response to hostile conditions. I met Hawass in the men's room of the Waldorf. He was holding this year's version of the Boston Psychoanalytic, the BPSI roster, up to the mirror to find the number of our own Leo Smyton, DDS. Hawass, ever the scientist, had discovered that every succeeding page of the roster was a stereoisomer of the preceding page, so that the pages could be read in sequence only with the aid of a reflecting surface. "See? Siner-Sipzenzer-Skinner-Smit ... unt ... *Smyton!*" Hawass pressed me to explain why we had abandoned the old roster format. "What was wrong with those cute little booklets? Like Beatrix Potter books. And always two unlabeled numbers for each name: office or home? analyst or spouse? A riddle. A crossroads." I explained how Diana had gotten caught up with Arnie Richard's new look-hip graphics-mixed fonts-cool colors *Journal of the American* that evoked the old guy with the makeup during the cholera epidemic in *Death in Venice*. I preferred the old *JAPA* because it was the exact color of gastric aspirate and because the layout was exactly the same as the *Freeport Boating News,* which listed the bluefish charters and carried an annual glossy of Guy Lombardo's natural wood racing boat with twin mercs.

Guy, our local hero, had an arrangement with the Jones Beach Musical Theater that he would conduct the Royal Canadians in the Schaefer tent every weekend night so long as his boat was included in every musical production at the theater—the theater stage was separated from the audience by a moat that communicated directly with the inlet. Leo Smyton was still in dental practice in Merrick in those days, and they had used his crown epoxy concoction to build and anchor the mountain for *The Sound of Music* out of plastic bricks. We went to the opening together, and I wanted Leo to appreciate with me the moment that Lombardo arrived by sea in the middle of the Alps with a racing boat full of Nazis to arrest the Von Trapps, but Leo was focused on the mountain, going on—in a loud voice that should have caused me some concern—about immutability and immortality. He was right, in a sense, because later on they couldn't budge his Alp without tearing up the stage, and so it had to be worked into the next year's production of *Pal Joey*, and then *Carousel*—they put a staircase on it for *Hello Dolly*—until the theater finally closed and his mountain was covered by drifts.

The Sphinx was covered by drifts for most of the past four thousand years until they dug it out in 1926, and it has been crumbling ever since. Zahi Hawass supervised repairs of the body with indigenous limestone and sand, but he refused to touch the nose because he said it would look tacky. When the project was finished and Hawass returned to New York, Smyton offered to bring him to Boston as the first recipient of our Visiting Academic Scholar outreach project.

There were other contenders: Some preferred Toril Moi, a statuesque Finnish English professor at Duke who reinterpreted the allegedly antifeminist Freud dictum "anatomy is destiny" to be a mis-understood Yiddish inflection joke derived from Napoleon's ironic cry, "*Politics* is destiny?!" Those of us who could see the emperor's clothes argued for a Lacanian woman from Berkeley who called her mother a "complex discursive event." And the nurturing sorts wanted to bring Eric Kandel back home to give him a corrective emotional experience. But Smyton argued convincingly and ultimately successfully for Hawass based on Hawass's paper "Evolution, Adaptation and Immortality," which Smyton misunderstood as "forward-looking." Then, after Jackie Zilbach accidentally knocked the nose off the Freud bust when she swung her staff—in jest, no doubt—at Gerry Adler dur-ing their animated discussion of the powers and limitations of a "pro tem" president, Steve Bernstein proposed the "Dysmorphology of the Immortals" program.

It began awkwardly but straightforwardly enough. Hawass told an apparently obscene permutation of the Sphinx riddle—four legs, two legs, three legs—with Clinton and Lewinsky, but then he got serious: how one hundred thousand peasants, driven from the fields by the late summer flooding, floated immensities of rock and limestone down the river in a makeshift work relief project—no mention by Hawass of Hebrew slaves, I assume for political reasons, or of Moses, except for his jokes about Jackie smiting the bust with her staff—one hundred thou-sand peasants, motivated to work beyond their immediate wants, beyond "the narrow capacity of the stomach," as Smith had it, by the illusions of an afterlife, illusions laid bare by Freud in the same 1926 when they re-exposed the Sphinx to the wear of the elements.

Then Smyton attacked.

"How do you respond to Professor Chikaosa Tanimoto of the

Kyoto University, whose forty research trips to the Giza Plateau have established that two-tenths of an inch of stone erodes from the chest of the Sphinx every year, leading inevitably to a destabilization of the neck and subsequent decapitation in the *near future* because you failed to use an epoxide resin with your limestone?"

Hawass said, "The future is infinite. How near can it be?"

Smyton: "You deny the prediction?"

Hawass: "Tanimoto is a self-aggrandizing fraud."

Smyton came back with his trump card, that Hawass's "authentic" limestone wasn't even from a Giza quarry. Then Hawass accused Smyton of bitterness owing to his exclusion from the all-Egyptian task force such that his synthetic additive—apparently and suggestively the same additive proposed by Tanimoto—received no serious consideration.

Their argument continued along familiar lines: How much change is necessary in order to survive, and at what point does your survival come at the cost of your identity? When does the Sphinx—already a composite of man and woman, lion and eagle, and sometimes a goat, depending on your myth—cease to be a Sphinx? When does it become a synthetic shadow of itself that will live forever to no other end?

Analysts, of course, recognize the terms of this debate—the Real and the Material versus the Symbolic and the Metaphorical—from the other major controversy that has preoccupied analytic circles this year: Should Clinton have eaten the wafer?

As you recall, Clinton was in Africa, the Presidential Penis was much in the news, the White House was considered to be diminished, but the polls were rising. The psychoanalyst Christopher Bollas got some press for his analysis of the public's sympathy for Clinton's misbehavior; an explanation stated more pithily by the comic Dennis Miller, who proclaimed, "What does it mean? It means that America loves blow jobs!" Then Clinton, a Southern Baptist, blew it himself by receiving Holy Communion at a Catholic Mass in South Africa. Now, the African bishops felt that they could give exception to a head of state, but the secretary for the Congregation of Divine Worship and the Sacraments, Vatican spokesman Bishop Geraldo Agnelo, said there could be no exception save in the case of "grave necessity and only if they accept that the Host is the *actual* body of Christ, not a mere symbolic representation." Apparently the priest who admitted the president to eucharistic communion, the Reverend Mohlomi Makobane, was more concerned that the Gospel reading for the day was about adultery. Makobane talked of inclusiveness. There was a tension between "outreach" on the one hand and "standards and identity" on the other. The Protestant denominations open their Communion table to Christians of all traditions, but the Catholic and Orthodox churches have a *stance* that reflects their *distinctive beliefs* about what *happens* at communion. Their certification of a recognizable Communion *process* helps distinguish between practitioners of the canon and Satan's helpers.

Freud thought that the riddle of the Sphinx was a thinly disguised mythological distortion of the riddle that causes the child to first become thoughtful, the riddle of where babies come from. Hawass takes the broader view whereby all Sufi paradoxes, Zen koans, obsessional dilemmas, and even the most pedestrian of contemporary analytic torments reduce to riddles on the roads to Thebes. Last year our analyst at the crossroads faced the riddle, "Once the analysts have disabused themselves of objectivity, authority, expertise, and a theory, why should anybody pay them for their time?" It was a *marketing* riddle that took us down a dead end. Even the most radical proponents of a softened, consumer-friendly psychoanalysis were given pause at the Committee on Public Relations when Smyton—impolitic, extreme, and inevitably misunderstood Smyton—proposed to Leon Hoffman's committee the media strategy, "We're not even *Jewish!*"

So this year's riddle is closer to home, or part of the search for home: "What does sex have to do with psychoanalysis?" Proposed a few years ago by Andre Green as a provocation, this question has been the theme in one form or another of every major national and international analytic conference in the past year. The problem is that analysts are having a bit of a problem remembering what sex is. When I asked some of our leaders whether sex is *back in* in psychoanalysis, they told me it isn't really sex, but something to do with the body in an interpersonal space. When I asked about cannibalism and incest and murder they said, "Those things happen too."

Are we still running from Freud's news about our nature? Are we really going to have to listen to how superficial we are and be taught the psychoanalytic facts of life by the French, for God's sake? Or are we still running *to* sexuality *from* meaning for the comfort of finding a coherent sense of ourselves in the mirror?

Which brings us to Viagra. Who needs to erect a whole pyramid? Who needs to promise an afterlife when more than half the men over forty in these United States complain of some form of erectile dysfunction? After the first million prescriptions were written, the People wanted to know more about the origins of their everyday happiness, they wanted a relationship, they wanted a *name.* And so they went to the Pfizer and asked, "Why '*Viagra*'"? But it turned out that it *meant* nothing. Not "Eureka!" Not Niagara Falls. Not Vigaro lawn fertilizer. Not "*vy aggra*vate yourself?" Not *vial*the route and *agra*/gravidarum. Just nothing. Well, not "just nothing," but an absolute studied meaningless-ness. An Internet search had been conducted on a scale that would be the envy of Pharaohs to find an inoffensive word that had meant absolutely nothing to any person, anywhere in the world, since the Sumerians first wrote with reeds on unbaked clay tablets. It stood, and will stand, as the birth of a new signifier, a complex discursive event, the Meaningless Erection.

———

I've been told that it's important to be adaptive. Don't get stuck in the past. Change is hard. Painful. As an outreaching educator of future physicians I received a new textbook of behavioral science to train students and physicians about *New Health Care Realities*. It had a chapter on "Managed Care and the Doctor Patient Relationship." The author, a full professor at a large medical school, said that doctors had less time to spend with patients, so it is important to create the *impression* that adequate time has been spent with patients. He believed in illusion. He recommended inserting strategic pauses . . . to create a sense that time has gone by. He recommended pacing your breathe-ing with the patient's breathe-ing, first slowly and then at an accelerated pace that moves them along . . .

An innovator came to our departmental grand rounds. He had received considerable funding to institute a mental health care delivery system in twelve American cities. One psychiatrist would supervise eight nurse practitioners; each nurse practitioner would carry a minimum of 90 psychiatric patients. The psychiatrist was responsible for 720 patients. He said there was a training program to standardize care. Each psychiatrist received training in the use of a wallet-sized laminated card that contained medication treatment algorithms. Each nurse received training in . . . "being there" . . . with the patient.

As I was sitting next to someone with the power to say whether I would continue to be able to serve as an outreaching educator of future physicians, I felt particularly motivated to demonstrate my capacity to embrace the future. I said to the visitor that this was, of course, an innovative approach to limited resources. I said that I imagined that if he had *unlimited* resources he would probably prefer that the doctor would *both* have the card *and* do the being-there with the patient, but he said "No." He said that there had been no controlled research trials—"no CRTs" is what he actually said—to support that position.

OK. So change is painful. So it's the *Seventh Seal* and we're up there in our robes on the hill, swinging our incense lamps.

When the plagues hit the Pharaoh it must have occurred to him at some point, even as the embodiment of Ra and Osiris and Lord of the Lower World, that he had somehow brought these things on Himself. The point is to be adaptive. Open.

At a discussion group at the December meetings of the American Psychoanalytic Association I listened to a group of psychoanalysts describe in the safety of the room that they had extrasensory powers and that people who still thought they lived in a world confined to three dimensions were to be pitied as "flatlanders," and then I went to a cutting-edge discussion group of analysts who said they used interpretations to prune neural networks and tweak the limbic system and that people who still dragged their feet on the mind-body problem were to be pitied as flatlanders, and then I went to a series of support groups for analysts so traumatized by their own analyses with analysts who never spoke to them or told them not to get married or buy a car or grow their hair that they pitied people who had yet to transcend aggression and generational conflict and called them flatlanders. I thought of the painting that had hung for months in the second-floor seminar room where I taught theory and where the candidates held their readings up to the reflective windows. It was a painting of a woman's torso wrapped in gauze with "NO EXIT" printed in block letters over her genitals. Leo Smyton had stood by the painting clutching his glue pot—he was helping Hawass with Freud's nose downstairs—and sniffed that we still tend to privilege the Body over Meaning, but I didn't think of "abandon all hope who enter here" or of "managed care penetration" or of any other somatic metaphor. I resisted the bourgeois tendency to fall into the illusion of the pictorial space within the frame. Instead, I thought of Freud's final reconsideration of religion in the *Outline* where he softened his view about religion—where he said there was truth in it, but the truth was not a material but a historical truth. Not an actual truth but a metaphorical truth, perhaps a symbolic representation of the truth.

My own beliefs may tilt away from the Papa on this point. For years in the Iglesia del Tren Subterranio I sat among the scriptures twice a day. Above me was a picture of a dark box that offered hope against powerful adversaries, against an infestation; beneath the box, the inscription to the enemy read, "SE PUEDE ENTRAR PERO NO SE PUEDE SALIR." You can enter, but you cannot leave. Depending on the day, I identified with the victor or the vanquished. And, at every door, a wider caution: "AVISO! La via del tren subterranio es peligrosa. Si el tren para entre las estaciones quedase adentro. No salga afuera!" "Attention! The subway tracks are dangerous. If the train stops between stations stay inside. Don't go out!"

Because it's cold out there.

Not just the care corporations can *manage* not to give . . . not just the flailings of psychoanalysis . . . but the unappreciated difficulty involved in dumbing down. Whatever the temptations to live forever as a plastic Sphinx in the desert, or to crumble on principle, once you have been encouraged to appreciate complexity and ambiguity and depth, it's hard to forget what you know. The entrances to the Pharaoh's chambers are one-way. Se puede entrar pero no se puede salir.

BPSI 1999
EMPIRICISM: THE TRAPPISTS

Now my co-mates and friends in exile
Hath not old custom made this life more sweet
Than that of painted pomp? Are not these woods
More free from peril than the envious court?

As fond as we are of good fellowship, we beat no retreat into the Wellesley woods this year but reached beyond our commonwealth and spoke in these days of good economy and rising practice to lawyers and toddlers and principals and teens and to the gentles and mechanicals of theater and film, canvas and verse.

My favorite moment of outreach came when Steven Cooper discussed the film *The Eel* at the Coolidge Theater. In language that was at once dexterous and accessible he elaborated an analytic reading of a story in which a man, emerging from years of imprisonment after killing his wife in a hallucinatory rage, is gradually brought back to the chance to battle with his unconscious through reparation and love.

A hand went up from the audience. "So what you are saying is that this PERP would be considered by psychoANALYSTS, to be OK, because his MURDER OF HIS WIFE was, like, an OEDIPAL THING?!"

Oh outreach … Oh community …
Sweet are the uses of adversity!

Another breakthrough moment for our society occurred when we pulled together to purchase a named sponsorship on the local public radio station. Day after day the newsreaders announced successive iterations of our identity. Sandwiched between the legal services of Jay, Wheeler, and Ditmar and the executive coaching offered by Jay Pomerantz associates, we heard of the "Boston Psychotherapeutical Society offering ... ," the "Boston Analytical Institute Offering Low Fee Society ... ," the "Boston Fee Low Society Offering Analytic Dough" ...

I enjoy our returns to Wellesley College. I consider myself an affiliate alumnus here because in 1972 my college allowed us, in what I understood to be a gender outreach program, to take a break from studies to participate in electoral politics. I spent the week here as an unofficial guest, where I sent the mail from the McGovern headquarters by day and represented the male at the newly constructed Schneider Student Center by night and where, in the midst of learning to send blood to my extremities until my fingers vibrated during an autogenics workshop, I was asked by my dorm mates to share my opinion about the Greta Garbo film *Queen Christina*, which had screened earlier that evening. I set the stage for my opinion by observing the use of the plot device in that film, so common in Shakespeare, of having the female protagonist assume a male disguise in order to observe, instruct, punish, and acquire the male.

A hand went up. "So what you are SAYING is that Greta Garbo cannot BE a man because of her BIOLOGY?"

My hand went to my face as I sought some words to say to avoid a scene. I could still feel my fingers pulsing with vibrations from the autogenics workshop. As I looked at her through my fingers she suddenly and inexplicably deescalated and simply gazed at me with no more thoughts of the social construction of gender.

Freud thought we had trouble with limits. And although he had a rather liberal view of the permissible, he could be strict in his observations of the running around we are inclined to do to pursue our love of shortcuts and the wish to have or be or do what we cannot. He skewered religious dogma as so much illusion based on the bad thinking of ignorant primitives backed by external coercion and bolstered by infantile longings. He dismissed the overreaching efforts of analysts to escape the limitations of themselves, their patients, or their technique as so much "misguided therapeutic ambition" based on more of the same.

His reality was nonnegotiable but open to discovery.

He believed, for example, in telepathy.

He confessed a sympathy for the "miraculous," and, although his actual experiments in telepathy while rooting around in the woods with Anna and Ferenczi looking for mushrooms were more secular, he allowed for the possibility of events at least as improbable as the prospects for McGovern's election that fall. The transmission of thought content through an invisible medium struck him as no more incredible than radio, and his observations regarding thought contagion in regressed groups and in the shared communications in the working colonies of insects anticipated Gilligan's similar theories regarding mentation in a syncitium of adolescent girls.

In the working colony of the women's dorm where I spent the week, the woman at the front desk, identified only as "Bells," would broadcast the aim and object of my arrival through the honeycombed hallways, through the transoms of room after room until it found the otic canal of the young woman in question. The messages were coded: the women were referred to as "visitors" and the men as "guests," and the communal defenses of the dorm were alerted by referring to any number of women accompanied by even a single male as the male plural "guests." On many occasions, I observed that during the moment just prior to the audible Bells transmission, the young women would suddenly and inexplicably look up at the open transoms above their doorways.

Earlier that very year it had been determined that the apparently degenerate organ, the cartilaginous external tympanum of aquatic turtles, was in fact adept at the perception of low-frequency sound waves. At my own school I was engaged in an experiment with three turtle women in which we attempted to train a series of aquatic turtles to seek food from an opaque, submerged petrie dish that was paired with a sound and not from the opaque dish that was not. By this means we attempted to discover whether turtles could hear with direction.

A problem developed. The turtles never moved. They never ate. After a few weeks taking shifts watching the turtles sit motionless in a four-foot-square Plexiglas tank filled with an inch of water, the three turtle women, as if responding to a signal that only they could hear, suddenly and inexplicably drifted away ... I was left to record the data alone. I was content to present data establishing that turtles don't eat. But on the final day of the final week of my observation of the static, starving turtles, each time I placed a turtle in the tank it suddenly and inexplicably scampered directly to the dish accompanied by the sound and gobbled up the food. There was no trial and error. No learning curve. They just knew.

I recently had the opportunity to mention these findings and observations to Guy Pinterra, a psychiatrist practicing in western Massachusetts who represents the extraordinary diversity that comes into our analytic community once we are willing to open the doors. Pinterra had been a Trappist monk in Guadalajara, then a noted herpetologist—"reptologist" to some—and a practicing iridologist and poikilotherapist before completing his medical studies and enrolling in the distance-learning psychoanalytic curriculum offered over the Internet by the New York Freudian Society. He became the representative of that correspondents study group to the consortium of allied groups seeking the title of "psychoanalyst" under a Massachusetts omnibus licensing statute currently in development. The consortium met at the Endicott House in Dedham, and I had occasion to speak with Pinterra during a guided tour of the gardens.

Pinterra pulls into his shell if he's not approached just so. He can be difficult; he feels unappreciated, perhaps with good cause. He listened silently as I described my findings from years ago, and he indulged me the story of my efforts to save our red-eared slider turtle, Jerry. Jerry, on being placed in a new tank, suffered a stress response that upset the balance of his immune system's ability to hold his commensal protozoa population in check. The resulting parasitosis was complicated by pseudomonas, a bacterial superinfection, that required me to inject an amino glycoside antibiotic into his pinioned foreclaw sixteen times over the course of two months while debriding necrotic shell fragments with tweezers and administering nightly surgical scrub baths with chlorhexiderm. The remission of his infection was complicated by anorexia, which I treated with tube feeding, and finally by torpor, which resisted my most stringent ministrations. The herpetologist now said that Jerry's recovery would require a miracle.

Pinterra said that he would answer my question once I had answered one of his own. "What is prerequisite for the meaningful study of psychoanalytic outcomes?" Fortunately, I had familiarized myself with Pinterra's writings and activities in anticipation of just such a moment. Specifically, I was familiar with Pinterra's article "Privileging Illusion" and with the source material for that article, namely, his appointment by the bishop of the Worcester Archdiocese to the troika investigating the claims of miraculous events in that region.

As a result of my researches, I knew of his emphasis on the importance of simulation in matters of faith such as scientific inquiry. He argues that the opposite of the truth is not a lie but a simulation of the truth. In his research, this position has led him to seek the perfectibility of control groups. In his faith, it derived from his participation in the anti-Augustinian movement among the Trappists, also known as the "scientists," the "anti-leapers," or just the "Guadalajara group."

In the late 1960s freethinking, pre-drug-culture, university-town ambiance of Guadalajara, the monks opened a silent dialogue with the local chapter of the Mexico City psychoanalytic society to collaborate on an inquiry regarding the nature of truth. They fastened onto two Freudian postulates. The first, from The Uncanny, was that *horror* is increased by presenting a world that is true, normal, and familiar in every particular except for the fact that it is known to be false. Hollywood had long capitalized on this observation with powerful results. The second, from The Future of an Illusion, was Freud's challenge to the faithful to make the data of religious belief accessible to any investigator who might care to pursue it, and "not only to the ecstatics." On the basis of these two postulates, the monks reconceptualized The Devil. They took the stance that faith does not require a leap of faith; it can be established empirically. The Devil was the control group for God.

The discussions with the analysts were initially restricted to correspondence because the monks were barred from speech by the sixth-century rule of St. Benedict that required them to seek contemplation in silence and separation. They ultimately received a special medical dispensation from the bishop that allowed them to talk in the privacy of psychoanalysis. The monks paid a price for opening their doors. The decision for analysis revived and enflamed local suspicions that the monks were, in fact, *Marranos*—swine, crypto-Jew descendants of the Spanish expulsion in 1492. The International Federation of Messianic Jews used the Trappist experiment to popularize their view that the majority of Hispanics from Mexico and Latin and South America were Marranos representing a sleeping giant of the diaspora that was beginning to stir. In California analytic circles, the rumor circulated that the monastery had closed within a year of the experiment because the monks abandoned the clergy when confronted with the unconscious aspects of their motivations.

Pinterra says that, in fact, only a couple of monks left. The actual diffusion of influence flowed in the direction of the analysts who were challenged by the Trappists to demonstrate the utility of psychoanalysis not as a matter of blind faith but by means of a meaningful outcome study. In the resulting research, patients at a mental health clinic, naïve to psychoanalysis, were randomized either to a control group analysis with a Trappist who offered written instruction regarding the fundamental rule but was otherwise silent, or to a supervised analysis with an analytic candidate who, given the times, spoke little more than the monks. Outcome data at twelve and eighteen months favored the Trappists but were not significant. Pinterra's article that appeared in *Revista de Psicoanalysis*, abstracted in the *Psychoanalytic Quarterly*—"*El uso de los Trapenses como Psicoanalistas Fingidos*" ("The Use of Trappists as Sham Psychoanalysts")—drew little comment outside Mexico because of suspicions about empirical studies. His argument that the study results were contaminated by a third-variable problem, that thought transference was a confounder, probably did not help his cause.

Years later, when Pinterra had left the monastery and was already well established as a herpetologist, he moved to the States to complete his medical studies at Washington University. Again the analytic community showed little interest in his research, but he felt at home at the medical school, where, in the absense of patients, faculty, and clinical facilities, a largely simulated curriculum based on hired actors and interactive computer programs provided him with ample opportunities to pretend to be a doctor. He channeled his analytic interests into the development of "poikilotherapy," a technique whereby an endotherm combines the abandoned Freudian techniques of mesmerism and pressure with heat and thought transfers to bolster the resiliency of ectotherms, that is, cold-blooded reptiles, primarily aquatic turtles.

All this passed through my mind in an instant. In response to his question, I said to him only this: "The Devil is a simulation of God."

He seemed satisfied. He said, "The young woman at the Wellesley Student Center deescalated by the same mechanism that the female *Pseudemys scripta* turtle is subdued for mating: the much smaller male vibrates the digits of his grossly elongated foreclaws before her eyes, thereby mesmerizing her in order to mount her *coitus a tergo,* as observed by the Wolfman. The warm-blooded feel they can learn nothing from the ectotherms. No matter.

"Auditory localization in aquatic turtles was worked out in the late 1980s by herpetological learning theorists who trained the turtles to withdraw their heads in response to sounds. The greatest sensitivity was noted in the range of 200 to 640 Hertz, which agreed quite closely with the direct recordings from the auditory nerve of the *Chrysemys picta*. The great leap forward in behavioral herpetology occurred when researchers stopped attributing complex subjective states to the turtles on the basis of naturalistic observations and began capitalizing on the natural repertoire of turtle behavior that could be influenced by environmental contingency. This strategy was later usurped by Daniel Stern and the infant observationalists without attribution. No matter."

Regarding the sudden and inexplicable evidence of thought transference, prescience, and telepathy in the dormitory, in the turtle tank, and among the turtle women, he said this: "First we must consider the locus of the occult. Freud, at the end of the nineteenth century, believed that the rising interest in the occult was a response to the threat posed to religion by the inexorable march of rational science. Now, at the end of the millennium, we find a rise in neuroscientific mysticism as a response to the threat to psychoanalysis posed by the inexorable march of rational market forces.

"Next, we must consider a context of meaning.

"Freud, like the Church, was concerned less with the likelihood of the paranormal—which he conceded—than with the why of it. He thought it made little difference whether individuals learned about their deeper selves through the disguised communications of a dream or through the tales of a fortune-teller. Freud was only concerned to demonstrate that the message continued to draw its power and meaning from the preoccupations of the unconscious.

"Similarly, the Church, since the time of Pope Benedict XIV in the eighteenth century, has emphasized the distinction between the merely paranormal and the miraculous. It is a distinction based on determining the theological foundations for the claims of the miraculous. The face of Jesus appearing in a tree is not a miracle—unless, perhaps, it saves the tree."

Working with the investigative team of the archdiocese, Pinterra saw the oils flowing suddenly and inexplicably down the walls of a home in Worcester, the sanguineous tears from a Madonna, the blood on a consecrated host, the healings and unexplained communications. All these could and would be subjected to scientific analysis, to laboratory tests of blood species and type, to brain scans, and the medical testimony would be delivered at the Vatican before the officially designated Devil's Advocate arguing against the Miraculous—but these analyses were not enough without consideration of intent, of motive, of meaning.

"Next week is the vernal equinox. *Nowruz*. The Iranian Islamic New Year. I have rooms at the cloister house of St. Joseph's Abbey. You may bring Jerry. We will attempt a poikilotherapy."

One week later in the woods abutting the cloister house, in the abbreviated habit assigned to guests, I helped Pinterra set up the *sofreh-ye haft-sinn*, the ceremonial cloth of *Nowruz*. On the cloth he placed a large bowl filled with water. In the bowl he placed a Seville orange to represent the earth floating in space and a goldfish to represent life. According to tradition, the orange would move at the exact moment of the equinox as Pisces moved into Aries. I commented on his eclecticism. He told me that the Islamic ritual enhanced his faith because all religions seek the same truth. I told him that our institute had opened its doors so wide that we were leaning toward expanding the free advertising that we provide in our society newsletter for our closest market competitors to include announcements from a group that was actively suing us before the patents and trademarks commission over our use of the term "psychoanalysis." I said that we sought openness and inclusiveness. He said that we deserved whatever happened to us.

"Taste this!" he said, shoving a cracker with a remarkably tasty marmalade into my mouth. "The monks at St. Joseph's Abbey are the first truly successful manufacturers of Seville orange marmalade. They did it by cooking their jam in a closed vacuum pan as opposed to an open kettle. The open kettle uses temperatures that are too high; it damages the fruit. By closing the pan, the monks achieved something distinctive and fragile."

Grasping Jerry tightly, one hand above the carapace, one hand below the plastron, he looked through his fingers into Jerry's clouded iris. Abruptly, he leapt with the tiny turtle back and forth over a small bonfire, all the while chanting, "*Sorki-e to az man o zardi-e man az to!*" ("Give me your beautiful red color and take back my sickly pallor!")

At exactly twenty-nine seconds past the forty-sixth minute past eight PM, the orange suddenly and inexplicably stirred, Jerry opened one brilliant emerald eye, scampered directly to the goldfish, and swallowed it whole, and Pinterra said:

> *"And this our life, exempt from public haunt*
> *Finds tongues in trees, books in running brooks,*
> *Sermons in stone, and good in every thing."*

BPSI 2000
PRAGMATISM: WATSON

I am pleased to have this opportunity to present to you our latest researches regarding the behavior of psychoanalysts in water. You will recall that our initial observations led us to describe a circular formation of analysts—arms linked, heads to the center, legs thrashing outward like sailors in shark-infested waters or like the agitated petals of a flower. It was a model that emphasized separation and vulnerability to a hostile surround.

In our second model, the polar heads of the analysts migrate to the periphery, where they interact with the charged dipoles of the water molecules. Legs are directed to the center of the micelle, where they mingle like the fatty acid tails of emulsified lipids washed by bile salts in the lumen of the jejunum. This model moves toward integration but falls short of our final model, the disc, in which analysts fall like drops of oil on a still water pool and spread in a concentric cascade that reaches an improbably large diameter, only limited by achieving a final uniform thickness across the disc of a single molecule.

The disc model combines the deconstruction of hierarchies with maximum outreach, but it has been criticized by those who would worry about the lack of depth in the analytic wafer, and about the relation of the most recent analysts to gambol toward splashdown over the heads of their immediate forebears to their earliest analytic origins.

These critics would say that in light of what Lewin, on the occasion of the twenty-fifth anniversary of the founding of the Boston Psychoanalytic Institute, in the year of Watson's passing, called our "spread," we risk losing contact with what John Murray called, on that same evening, that "unique something" in psychoanalysis and what Menninger called our "compass." These critics would say that, in our pursuit of an open culture of learning, we now make committees rather than contributions. And they would quote Sylvia Pojoli's husband, the well-traveled Roman journalist who, when asked about the difference between Moscow and Rome, said that in Moscow they know nothing about what's going on but understand everything and in Rome, they know everything but understand nothing. So, they say, we, with all our committees, talk with each other. We know everything that's going on—everything on the road from Moscow to Rome.

Surely these critics fail to appreciate the complex relationship between science and marketing. Freud was an inspirational leader, but his skills as a market strategist were limited to mitigating the consequences of anti-Semitism. He asked Carl Jung to put a gentile face on the psychoanalytic message. Jung was so enthralled with his role as heir that he enthusiastically shared with Freud his observations both of the poltergeist that he believed to possess Freud's desk and of various matters pertaining to the Aryans, including his discussion of Aryans buried in the bogs around Bremen where Freud, Jung, and Ferenczi waited for the German steamer that would carry them to the United States.

Regarding the bodies buried in the Bremen bogs, Freud detected a death wish in Jung's remarks and fainted. Regarding the possession of his office furniture, Freud said that he could not hear the sounds but then regretted introducing this note of alienation with his new Crown Prince and assured Jung that he *did* believe that his telephone number—14362—contained a prognostication of his own death between the ages of 61 and 62, although Rosensweig argues that Freud used this number only as an apotropaic to ward off the evil in an earlier number—2467—that connected Freud both to the now abandoned Fleiss prediction that Freud would die at the age of 51, and to the about-to-retire General E. M., who once punished the 24-year-old Freud, returned, and thereby caused Freud's episode of nervous illness at 30, and served in Freud's idioverse as the precursor to the Cruel Captain that used the story of the Rat Torture to excite and torment the Rat Man, with whom Freud was therefore, at the inframediate level of his idiodynamics, one and the same, minus the rat.

When they got to New York, Jung again broached things Aryan on a walk with Freud in Central Park. Shortly afterward, traveling on Riverside Drive, Freud suffered one of his embarrassing episodes of incontinence that Jung attributed to ambition and that Patrick Mahoney attributes, on this occasion, to Freud's view of the Palisades across the river because the "palus" suggests pole, stake, or poker—just as my friend Andy Parker, known, in fact, as Mr. Poker to the campers in his charge, frequently assured them that "enuresis is nothing to be ashamed of."

On a third occasion, with the split a *fait accompli,* Freud needed to confront Jung about Jung's repeated failure to footnote Freud and fainted again. Jung carried the smaller man to a couch where Freud dreamily spoke of "how sweet it must be to die." So, from a marketing perspective, a mixed result at best.

There are those, however, who intuitively grasp the connections between science and marketing that can prove so elusive to the psychoanalyst. Consider these examples:

At a party in Marin County, north of San Francisco, an attractive young woman awash in Indian cottons and turquoise asked me about the chemical equations she spied on a T-shirt underneath my coat.

"What's that?" she asked.

"The Krebs cycle, the final common pathway to obtain energy from fuel molecules."

"What's a Krebs?"

"Hans Krebs worked out the pathway. He won the Nobel Prize for it. In fact, right now, he's working at Berkeley."

She seemed impressed, but a moment later something occurred to her that impressed her even more.

"Oh!" she said, "and does he make the shirts?"

At the Columbia College of Physicians and Surgeons, a packed auditorium of first-year medical students awaited the arrival of a lecturer who would begin to unlock the mysteries of psychiatry. A man in a long white coat bulled his way to the podium. He ripped from his coat a book with a green cover and held aloft a copy of the *Diagnostic and Statistical Manual in Psychiatry*, 3rd edition. "I want to tell you about a book," he said with some urgency, "that is not only the most important book in the history of psychiatry but ... an international best seller!"

A recent grand rounds presentation about the use of behavioral flooding to treat phobic avoidance consisted, in large part, of the presentation of two twenty-minute segments of network television news entertainment programs in which an attractive male reporter, in an open-collared shirt, accompanied people suffering from phobias through their treatment program. The people said they were afraid. A woman who had been a beauty contestant stayed in her room at home. A man who had played soccer had to be delivered onto an airplane drunk, in a wheelchair. They were assigned a young, attractive female therapist who told them to face their fears. At first they didn't want to, but then they did. She told the woman who was afraid of enclosed places to go *into* an elevator, so she did. She told the man who was afraid of open spaces to go *into* a field, so he did. Then the woman went to a mall, which was an open space, but she seemed happier. And the man jumped out of an airplane while mounted onto the back of a male instructor in a suggestive position. The man was very excited and gave a thumbs up that suggested that he was happier too. The presenter said that they got a lot of calls after the television broadcasts. He said that they thought the treatment would take three weeks but that the news magazine had asked them to cut the treatment to eight days because that was all the time they had to film the segment, so now they offer an eight-day treatment, Sunday to Monday, for $2500, not including transportation or room and board or extras like buying things at the mall or jumping out of a plane.

The young woman marketer, the professor of the celebrity book, and the grand rounds television presenter all appreciated the close relationship between claims for one's science and merchandizing. But psychoanalysts have been slow to grasp the concept despite continuous reminders to enhance both their research and their outreach. Perhaps the problem has been the tendency of analysts to treat the two concerns of science and the marketplace separately.

Almost a century ago, John Broadus Watson observed from behind the grocery counter at Macy's that the two concerns are really one and the same when he celebrated—discovered, really—the homology of form between the learning curves of his rats and the sales curves of his marketed commodities.

As an undergraduate, I was similarly moved, by the formal similarity between the dive and bob-turn lap-swimming behavior of the Freudian analysts at our university pool and the runway bar-press behavior of my rat Broadus in the experiment that I was completing in the animal laboratory. I was a lifeguard, and I watched them each day as I sat with William Octavius Bowser—the custodian from South Carolina who alternately pushed pigs and tobacco as reliable cash crops and helped me to consider the motivations of analysts in terms of their faith—and Tony Melos—my behaviorist friend whose insights were facilitated by the government-grade hallucinogens left over in the syringes he used in the lab to induce stereotyped circling behavior in rats.

Melos considered arguments built on homologies of form to represent primitive modes of thought.

I took his point, but how could I account for the fact that, in his later years, Watson liked to stand by the windows of his skyscraper office and stare down at the pedestrians far below who scampered the sidewalks like runways on the way to their rodent labors? Was it merely the *"compliance of chance"*? Or that Melos's own brisk barefoot walks—modeled, as they were, on the *zests* Granville Hall recommended to Freud as a remedy for intestinal cramps, and punctuated at the terminus by pushups—*seemed as uncomfortably familiar as Freud's buried spring that suddenly comes to ground?*

Melos also objected to observing phenomena like the swimming analysts naively, or "pseudo-naively," as he called it. He was, at the time, particularly sensitized to willful misunderstandings by the recently released Frederick Wiseman film about the Yerkes primate lab that showed the researchers causing excited male chimps to ejaculate into Plexiglas tubes. He felt that the viewing public *was not in a position to evaluate* the images and that Wiseman's claim to be "just pointing the camera" was disingenuous.

Yerkes had been Watson's Fleiss. At the nodal points of Watson's scandal-pocked career he looked to Yerkes for counsel. After the rat scandal, Watson wrote to Yerkes from his post observing snooty terns in the Dry Tortugas to say that until psychologists were identified with zoologists, they would never receive respect.

After Watson's father vanished into the woods for the last time, Watson's mother sold the farm to bring her son to Greenville, South Carolina, hoping to make him into a preacher. But he was arrested, instead, for beating up blacks and shooting off rifles, and it wasn't until she died that he made it to the University of Chicago and tried to determine what special senses rats need in order to learn by surgically removing one sense after another in experiments so gruesome that editorials appeared as far away as the *New York Observer* calling for his arrest as a torturer of rats.

It was a sex scandal, however, that drove him from Chicago to Johns Hopkins, where the chairman who recruited him was also caught in a sex scandal involving the local bordello. And so, at 31, Watson became chair of his department at Johns Hopkins, and at 36 he was elected president of the American Psychological Association and recognized as the undisputed leader of the behaviorist juggernaught in American psychology. His wife, however, refused him sex—he felt that she could be helped only by Freud—and so he started a new affair with his graduate student. He was very excited. The two of them went into a room and banged pots and pans over the head of a 9-month-old infant boy and a white rat. In this charged primal atmosphere, the infant displaced his anxiety onto the rat and became famous. Watson was not as fortunate. The affair was discovered, and his wife's powerful family had Watson's love letters published in the *Baltimore Sun*. He was thrown out of Hopkins overnight. He ended up at the advertising firm of J. Walter

Thompson, where, as a new hire, he served a series of clerkships peddling Yuban coffee and rubber boots before his stint behind the grocery counter at Macy's. After he was fired, Yerkes was the first to line up for his old job at Hopkins. Melos says that it always comes back to Darwin.

Watson was philosophical about the sex scandal. He credited Freud with recognizing that what we know as affection is merely a conditioned emotional response derived from a stimulation of the sexual organs, specifically the tumescence and detumescence of the genitals that many believed Watson sought to measure with a box of instruments discovered at Johns Hopkins that has long been rumored to be the true cause of his dismissal—although Professor Buckley notes that the instruments were not introduced by his wife's attorney as part of the divorce proceedings and that they resist a clear interpretation of their function.

Melos felt that my interest in Watson was misguided and that rather than looking for homologies of form, we should be looking for the points of disturbance from which an infinite variety of vectors spread in what appear to us to be concentric waves. Darwin, he argued, dropped such a pebble in our pond.

Among the responders, Granville Hall, Inviter of Freud, attacked Darwin to promote the new profession of psychology. He said that the new experimental science would reestablish the Divine line between man and the animals. Freud embraced Darwin to support his attack on religion; he collapsed phylogeny into the unconscious. Watson embraced Darwin to support his attack on humanity; he said human consciousness didn't exist because he could not see or feel it. Asked if mental states—thought, perception, cognition, feeling—had anything to do with human behavior, he said that the only mental activity of interest to the psychologist is the observable and measurable vibration of the larynx. We talk to ourselves and mistake our soliloquies for internal worlds.

As the ripples spread across the pond, the bobbing of any given point can be plotted over time but no single graph can capture the motion of all the points. With time, the inner rings become still, the disc becomes a doughnut, and the past an extrapolation. We bob as the wave passes through us for a moment; we impose our present on all that memory is.

And so, Tom Willis, of the Creation Science Association for Mid-America, restores a Victorian order for the Kansas State Board of Education by ghostwriting the new laws outlawing the teaching of evolution except in the microsphere. And humans, as described in the Most Important Work in the History of Psychiatry, which is also an International Best Seller, are categorized by the vibrations of their larynxes. And the mental states refined by Freud are left to the animals . . . who won a case last year when the United States Court of Appeals for the District of Columbia Circuit gave a zoo visitor at the Long Island Game Farm Park and Zoo the legal standing to sue the government so that Barney, a chimpanzee, could be united with Samantha, also a chimp, in a neighboring cage. The suit is still being fought in federal court, although Barney, as reported by Glaberson, was shot to death in 1996 after escaping, biting someone, uprooting a sign, and throwing it at a merry-go-round. The lawyers argue that *animals* are sentient beings with perceptions, cognitions, and emotions. Steven M. Wise, champion of chimps and bonobos, is currently fighting in a Massachusetts appeals court to compensate not just the property loss but also the emotional distress of the owners of seven pet sheep murdered by a neighbor's dog. Wise argues that the relationships were well developed. The sheep owners, a taxidermist and his wife, let the sheep in the house and baked them muffins.

I was proud that my rat's implant was successful enough that he would live out his days in the lab pressing his bar for all comers. But I cannot say that I am a rat person. Rat people think of rats as house dogs: smart and rather clean under the right circumstances. Rosensweig thought Freud was a rat man but he was a dog man. In the Jewish bible, the dogs are symbols of male prostitutes but there is no mention of cats at all because they are identified with the Egyptians, who deified them after importing them from Libya to kill rats. Cats were killed in Druid ceremonies because the static electricity from their fur proved they were satanic. And they have long been eaten throughout Asia, but Phan Van Khai, the prime minister of Vietnam, recently outlawed serving cat in restaurants and exporting them for food to China because the rat population has exploded during the warm El Niño weather and is eating half the rice crop, and, although the central province farmers claim to kill as many as three and a half million rats per week, their numbers continue to grow. And so the rats and cats continue to chase each other around the world in what might be considered one of the microevolutionary struggles still acceptable in Kansas.

My wife is allergic to cats. In fact she is an ailurophobe, a cat phobic. She believes that she knows if cats have ever been present in a given environment or whether they ever will be. Cat antigen number one, a protein secreted in cat saliva that dries on their fur when they clean themselves and is released as dander, is, in fact, the most potent antigenic stimulus we know. I told my wife that Stekel concluded that ailurophobes, typically women, suffer from homosexual fears when faced with this symbol of female sexuality, but she was unmoved. I told her that S. Weir Mitchell had convincingly argued against the racial memory hypothesis that attributed the phobia to trace traumas with saber-toothed tigers; he said it was asthma. But she had stopped listening.

When I presented my wife's case and those of my atopic children at the pet store they offered me a hypoallergenic rat. I pitched the rat as a house dog that giggled. Of course you could not hear the giggle, but Jaak Panksepp and Jeffrey Burgdorf of Bowling Green State University in Ohio had determined that rats possess a high-pitched, chirping whistle-giggle outside the range of human hearing by which they communicate their discrimination between playful and threatening physical behavior. My wife, however, was caught up in one of her many attempts to explain evolution to our alarmed 6-year-old.

"You were a monkey?" my child asked.

I had no better luck with our 10-year-old. I was telling her how the salt content in our extracellular fluid echoes the seas from which the first unicellular life emerged, and she, fresh from the planetarium, says, "I thought we were 'star stuff'!" I give her the primordial sea and she comes back with the Big Bang. I give her homologies; she comes back with the wave.

Freud's ripple ended in 1939. Chased from his own country by killers, he had to contemplate once again the lengths to which people would go to maintain their illusions of control. The psychoanalytic wave rolls on, threatened only by its own success and the endless temptation to become sensible.

Watson's ripple ended in 1958. He built his success as an advertising executive on the insight that doubt can be cultivated and new behaviors reaped through the testimony of professed experts. He went on radio to convince people that the way to have sex appeal is to smoke and the way to smoke without bad breath is Pebeco toothpaste, and from this pyramid of suggestion he reached for a society of social engineers armed with behaviorist technologies who would replace teachers, government officials, clinicians, and mothers. And, in the end, while living out his days as a recluse in a shack simulation of his Carolina origins tucked *heimlich* into the Connecticut woods, with only alcohol and his outdoor rats to keep him company, he speculated on who would have to die—what deviants, recalcitrants, and nonresponders—to maintain the order of his more perfect world. The behaviorist wave rolls on, fueled by our endless thirst for prediction, control, and efficiency.

I carefully lifted Broadus into the starting box and fitted a fine wire socket to the electrode that passed through his wax skull cap into his lateral hypothalamus. The wire rose to a ceiling pulley so that Broadus could run unencumbered from the starting gate to the bar. I controlled the separate currents that primed the speed of his run at one end and rewarded the frequency of his bar press at the other. In this way, I had my hand on the throttle of both his drive and his gratification.

But once, in this triangle of wire and pulley that defined his world and firmament, after I pushed the button to prime his charge, he paused just a moment and glanced in my direction—for a rat, too, may look at a king—and as he scampered down the runway toward his ultimate reward, an inaudible, invisible cackle whistled and chirped through the lab like a spreading pool of oil, searching for someone with enough larynx to appreciate the joke.

BPSI 2001
INCLUSIVENESS: THE NUNS

No Papist ruminations this year about trying to hold on to who we are and what we do during these diffusing days of marketplace science, no sir. Please indulge me with a few moments for personal housekeeping notes.

Earlier this year Party Spokesperson Joan Wheelis called me on the telephone. She asked me to talk tonight. I was honored but said no. The doorbell rang. It was Joan Wheelis. She asked me to talk tonight. I said that I had other commitments this year. Joan wagged a finger in my face. I said a scolding was unnecessary. She said that she was not scolding me. She said she was performing EMDR, an eye movement technique, to free me of whatever trauma was inhibiting my participation. Joan is pragmatic. I said, "I have no time to prepare and I am not going to stand in front of a wall of faces with nothing but my program in my hand." Joan moved her finger from right to left and from left to right. I said, "Talk to the hand, Joan." Joan said that I must "face the wall."

I remembered the wall. My father, a military reservist between the wars, saw life in our family barracks as an opportunity to practice creative anachronism. He did not hear my early verbalizations as the *anlage* prefigurations of later monologues, he heard them as an opportunity for discipline, and so I spent segments of my development facing a wall. That Joan's pre-relational "face the wall" finger appeared to apprehend this moment of my early history was not entirely surprising, and, well, here we are.

So, in very brief:

BPSI outreach had a remarkable year. We were in the newspapers. We were the focus of national conversation. We found topics that actively engaged our membership.

Nationally the number of psychoanalysts reportedly dropped another 1 percent and the average age of the membership rose to 63. Marketers have encouraged us to approach new audiences with a less forbidding product such as occurred when teenage "popera" sensation Charlotte Church topped the Billboard charts with a selection of crossover hits that sold in the millions and reversed a malaise caused by the downward spiral of classical music sales. Paul Burger, president of Sony Music Entertainment Europe, said that only the "classical cognoscenti ... a small ... but, regrettably, closed community," felt the successful outreach was limited by the fact that the recordings are not, in fact, opera.

In a related development, the Sisters of St. Joseph in Mt. Holyoke, facing dwindling recruits and an aging membership, discovered that many more women would be interested in becoming nuns if they could do so part-time, without celibacy, interference with a career, or other inconveniences. Some have argued that this solution to the vanishing vestals will defeat the point of the religious life, that it is the task of the religious community sisters to help the lay members of the church. But the lay members want to be sisters too, and so now they will work in the convent as "temporary sisters." In this way the mission may outlive the missionaries, and it will remain a question as to the importance of the fact that the new, so-convenienced sisters are not, in fact, nuns.

And there was comfort and commiseration as well for our friends under the Smith Kline umbrella, the American Psychiatric Association, who discovered their doppelganger in two groups with a history of pro- gressive ideals that have insisted that drug money is necessary for their operations and for the preservation of their mission. The groups, the Columbia Revolutionary Armed Forces (FARC) and the National

Liberation Army (ELN) inherited their drug money from the government-sponsored dismantling of the for-profit Medellin and Cali cartels. Asked whether this arrangement might corrupt the ideals of these people's movements, journalist Mark Bowden said that the movements had never convinced the populace of their worth and that forty years was a long time to live in the mountains.

So tonight we will party, dance, and spin again. My limited participation will be supplemented by the creative contributions of our other speakers. Rachel Seidel will at long last perform her interpretive dance based on the epic of Gilgamesh. Elliot Schildkraut and Jeffrey Nason will perform their interpretation of the Karen and Richard Carpenter song "Close to You." And President-Elect Leonard Glass, an instructor in the now famous BPSI Ethics Curriculum, will not speak, but I just get a kick out of mentioning him.

BPSI 2002
TRANSPARENCY: TARANTELLA

As you have, no doubt, heard, there will be no dancing tonight. Concerns were expressed. It was a decision taken up in committee. It was not an open process. News leaked out. There were rumors that the decision was influenced by the impromptu conga line at last year's event and by the exaggerated reports of the Nason-Glass tarantella that brought the evening to a close. My understanding is that these events were mentioned only in passing. Regarding the general issue of exhibitionism, the committee was guided by Ernst Kris, who acknowledged that "Our expectations are significantly limited when we hear that a certain patient is a ... dancer," that we "expect certain typical conflict constellations" around "coping with exhibition," but he cautioned that the success or failure of the therapy will be determined by the relative autonomy of the "dominant wish" and the conflict that turned proclivity and interest in that particular direction.

No. The deciding issue was mass hysteria. Mass hysteria and the need for confinement. In the *danse macabre*, the ecstatic dance, the dance of death, at the outset of the Middle Ages, the people gathered in the churchyards to dance and sing while the representatives of the church tried in vain to stop them. The church leaders enacted but failed to recognize the important role played by this very containment *in the dance* and thereby led to the next iterations of the *danse* that emphasized hierarchies of power and an escalation of hysteria.

The allegorical *danse* of death that evolved, the *Totentanz*—captured in the woodcuts designed by Han Holbein the Younger and executed by Hans Lurtzelburger, the woodcuts vaguely discernible in the frieze of the institute library, the woodcuts that inspired Nason and Glass—depicts a Great Procession of humanity, scrupulously ranked "from Pope and emperor to child, clerk, and hermit." In the Procession, the Living are led by the Dead to the Equalizing Grave. And all are summoned to repentance, regardless of privilege.

In Holbein's woodcut, Death's tap on the shoulder is not just democratic. It is also a surprise. It catches the people unawares in the midst of their daily life—much as my tap made Glass jump when I approached him from behind in the institute parking lot—he had set up a folding chair by the carpool space garbage cans and used yellow police tape to demarcate his territory. Our lot has been a perennial site of disorder in which a loosely defined group of the privileged parkers gather to honk, park, bang, and screech while a group of institute leaders attempt in vain to stop them.

In a remarkable if unappreciated document that gathered its inspiration not from the Friend's Service Committee polemics against the war so favored by Nason but from the *Enchiridion Militic Christiani* (The Handbook of a Christian Knight) by the great humanist Erasmus, who railed against institutional authority and reminded us that "monasticism is not piety," Glass, Our Servant, implored us to be better than ourselves and to gather in a progressive rationing of communal space and resources.

He was derided for his vision and now sat alone among his pails. Diana offered to spell him, but when she arrived outside, the "ool" had torn off his carpool signage and she lacked the fortitude to sit labeled as a fish. "Why a 'Carp'?" she tried to ask, but her voice was drowned out by the din of Nason, that Seeker of Truths, hammering his Ninety-Five Theses to the door like Luther at Wittenburg. Luther's challenge to papal authority, inspired by Erasmus, led to the iconoclastic riots, pan censorship, and a suppression of the arts that sent Holbein fleeing to Erasmus in England in that same year that he completed the design of the *Totentanz* woodcuts.

In Germany, the *Totentanz* inspired danced dramas. In Italy, the resurgent *danse macabre* inspired ecstatic death dance frenzies of convulsive sweating, frothing screams, and leaps that were so pervasive as to constitute a public menace. The frenzies were explained away as an epidemic of *tarantism*—the syndrome, a mass hysteria, in the time of the Black Death, mistakenly attributed to the bite of the venomous spider.

Holbein the Younger sat in England painting portraits of Erasmus, More, and the King, and designing royal robes and livery. His portraits presented a paradox of two-dimensional form and illusionist depth. He appeared equally detached from Matters of Spirit and the Turmoil of Events around him. He was a *watcher*. But was not his remove at the same time a part of the very *Totentanz* that he chronicled in such exquisite detail? To paraphrase Glass's fondness for the military reservist's creed, "They also serve who only stand and watch." And so we ask, is there really to be no dance tonight? Just because everyone is watching an empty dance floor? Certainly, the recent conga line of presenters that cycled through the packed auditorium of the members seminar did not suffer from the impossibility of separating the watchers and watched.

Which brings us to our experiment: Like the bite of the maligned tarantula, this exercise may be painful but not dangerous—and what if it were? The tarantella, that tame legacy of St. Vitus and the tarantists, is a folk dance performed by couples. It consists of light, quick steps and teasing, flirtatious behavior to lively six-over-eight-time music. Women dancers typically carry tambourines. The tarantists believed that their illness—weeping and skipping, leading to a wild dance—was also the cure, by which they distributed and disposed of the toxin through sweat. The Nason-Glass tarantella was a more subdued affair, befitting their responsibilities as president and president-elect of our society but underlining their sympathy for the institutional issues of power and privilege and an agenda for progressive social order. We honor them now with the toast of a gestural verse, an imagined band, a tarantella homage to the *Totentanz*, the democratizing touch of the Reaper, and Communal Drives:[1]

> *Nason and Glass*
> *Glass and Nason*
> *One with a Rhyme*
> *One with a Reason.*

> *Glass and Nason*
> *Nason and Glass*
> *Everyone's touched*
> *No one is passed.*

---

[1] J. Wheelis and A. Celenza, tambourines and dance

BPSI 2003
HUMILITY: PLIMOTH

I suppose we should start with the pigs.

In Borneo, gynecocracies of bearded pigs are sustained by fruit scraps dropped by societies of orangutans living in the rain forest canopy.

No one called me this year. Usually I get a call sometime in February to start thinking about the spring party. It occurred to me that last year's *Totentanz* tarantella homage to the Nason-Glass echoes of Erasmus and Holbein might have been inadvertently understood, which would, well, explain a lot. But a couple of weeks ago, just in case someone in the party committee star chamber was assuming something that would lead to a last second surprise, I figured I should leave a message for Diana. Diana, with whom I would estimate conservatively I have spoken twice a day for fifteen years, returned my call with her signature introduction, "This is Diana Nugent of the Boston Psychoanalytic Society and Institute." My mother, who also hesitates to make presumptions about our relationship, begins messages, "It's just your mother . . . ," but even my mother does not feel obligated to use her full name and address. I said, "Diana, after all these years, couldn't you say, 'This is *Diana* of the Boston Psychoanalytic Society and Institute?' and Diana said, "We are looking forward to hearing you this year," and I said, "Well, that is funny because I have been looking forward to hearing from you this year," and Diana said many things with some urgency of which I could only make out the words "February" and "Joan Wheelis" and then she hung up.

Joan called that evening and initiated her performance of faux-submission and seductive cajoling while her troops massed at my borders.

We both knew I would do what she asked because I like to, and because I am, well, scared of her. I owed it to my analysis to say something about the late notice, and Joan, who is very "big firm," denied fault, denied lateness, and said the lateness was my fault because I should know, and because she was only saving me work, and because she was good and I was bad and I should be happy to know her at all. All of this is undoubtedly true, but my ritual with Joan has, in fact, drifted over the years, ever closer to the date of the scheduled celebration—an asymptotic trend that has steadily reduced my preparation and production and, thereby, has represented the drive toward silence that Freud attributed to our longing for the peace of our inorganic origins. The oscillation between the shrinking length of the notice and the heat of the invitation evokes the Freudian dualism between the quest for entropic death and erotic trends seeking to unite the immortal germ cells—germ cells whose species-preserving conception and mitotic cleavage represent the first structure formation and mirror the crack that has recently spread like a dark stain across the ceiling of the library that threatened to come down on the head of our librarian Vivian Goldman like so much falling sky.

We're broke. Once again we must talk about selling the building and taking to the fields just as the pilgrim Saints of the Holy Discipline eschewed all houses of worship to pray with Bradford in Plimoth sheltered only by God's firmament.

Last year we had our Chicken Little troubles and evoked the *Totentanz*, but this year the war, the recession, the plague, and the endless winter were more than balanced by the happy developments whereby Dr. Melfi received further accolades from the American Psychoanalytic Association, the ApsaA, and whereby Stewart Cink, the golfer, attributed his precipitous rise on the PGA money list and his second-round lead at the MCI Heritage Classic to his psychoanalyst, Preston Waddington.

Scott Gardner, chair of the American Psychoanalytic Association Public Information Committee, was disturbed, however, to discover that a picture of Freud with a cigar continues to decorate the home page of the ApsaA. While he conceded that Freud remains a "big factor for those interested in psychoanalysis," he said that the cigar is very unappealing and recommended obtaining a consultation on this point from Andrea Schettino, the designer of the new ApsaA logo.

What is in an image? Does it give us what we require? Does it lose its meaning when it dissolves into another thing?

I once listened to Jean-Luc Godard, as he drew upon the cultural tradition that brought intersubjective deconstruction to full flower, in order to patiently explain to a distressed and soon to be baffled viewer of Godard's agitprop film—a film that pairs an image of Golda Meir with the voice of Adolf Hitler—that the viewer was disturbed because he was mistaking light passed through pieces of spliced cellophane for the things-in-themselves. "An image of an apple," Godard said, "is not an apple." The architect Michael Graves, on the other hand, before he took to designing beautiful appliances for Target that do not work, suggested a different solution to the question of the relationship between a thing and its representation; a solution that may be useful to us in our building deliberations. Graves addressed the limitations in his patrons' resources and in existing methodologies by designing structures that were intended to be realized only in watercolors. He designed buildings you could hang on a wall. Jeremy Gilbert-Rolfe, my visual arts instructor, told me not to bother with Graves because architecture would never be a true art form, lacking, as it did, a capacity to generate its own avant-garde. Michael Mahoney—the Kuhnian philosopher of science, not the Freud scholar—told me that psychoanalysis would never be a true science, lacking, as it did, a means of verification through experimental research.

This perennial charge was frequently in the literature last year with regard to institutional structures and hierarchies in light of the more general question about the stability of the analytic sky.

Ernst Kafka, who likes buildings with more than one story, said that some analysts are more informed about psychoanalysis than others, thereby providing a basis for evaluations and distinction among peers. Paul Mosher, a building leveler, responded that in a nonexperimental science, individual experiences are the only data and that psychoanalysts, and all their attempts at judgments, must, therefore, defer to what he called the "genius of the whole." A local bomb thrower opined that Kafka was a plantation owner fighting for slavery. (Last year he would have been described as a Nazi or pro-Vietnam warmonger, but divisions among the anti-authoritarians with regard to Iraq have made these militarist analogies problematic.)

In a different sector, Rubin and Zarumski of Wash Limbaugh University in St. Louis, wrote in *Academic Medicine* that psychotherapy, and psychological approaches, could no longer be considered a part of psychiatry; rather, psychiatrists should be clinical neuroscientists with "communication skills."

However, Raymond Rohner, the Swiss animal behaviorist, observed that "there are moments in research when the question as to what is truth and what is fiction becomes irrelevant." As described in the annals of the APSA—this would be the Australian Pig Scientists Association and not the American Psychoanalytic Association—we learned that Rohner founded Pig Vision in 1993 to encourage interdisciplinary collaborations in the arts and the sciences. One such collaboration set the switch button of a pedestrian traffic light in a piggery in Australia and linked it via the Internet with a set of traffic lights in Europe so that pigs in Australia literally stopped traffic in Europe—which, I think, explains a lot.

The ApsaA is coming to Boston next month—the analysts, not the pig scientists. Before the meetings begin, wall painting analysts from around the country will spend days of lost income sequestered in the stale air of hotel room suites pushing paper in thankless committee tasks for which they are traditionally rewarded by the host city institutes with a token reception—until this year, when a proposal was made to resist the temptation to suck up to these bishops, these representatives of the gross darkness of popery with their vile ceremonies and unprofitable canons and decrees: not to buy these old serpents of lordly and tyrannous power so much as a drink, but to devote our resources to worthier causes.

The proposal was greeted with acclamation and a chorus of Huzzahs! The announcement that our brethren at PINE planned to join us in this uprising led to further pandemonium—right up to the moment of our declaring our intent to the executives of the ApsaA, at which point PINE bailed and announced its own party and we were left standing with only our fruit scraps in our hands.

Some say we proved, thereby, that our pettiness was exceeded only by our ineptitude. But our aspirations to smallness undoubtedly played well on the psychoanalytic street, and the money we saved allowed us to join the representatives of the American meeting Arrangements Committee on the scouting trip for the larger planned outing for ApsaA meeting registrants to Plimoth next month.

Richard Bluestone, our guide, was a retired social worker and member of the General Council of the SCA—the Society for Creative Anachronism, not the Sexual Compulsives Association. At the Plimoth Colony, he performs the role of Governor William Bradford. On the bus, Bluestone had ample time to describe his SCA alter persona, Sir Thomas Blystock the Just of Carolingia, Chief Alchemist at the regional Renaissance Faires, during our long wait in traffic on Route 44 while accidents were cleared that had been caused by a sudden, inexplicable plague of malfunctioning traffic lights.

Bluestone tends to conflate the lexicons of his two, actually three, worlds—he has been known to appear at the Thanksgiving festivities with a tankard and belt pouch swinging from his doublet and breeches and, on one occasion, forgot to unbraid his beard. Regardless, his pitch tying alchemy to psychoanalysis goes as follows: In the alchemic situation, the burning of the prima materia through a process of calcination in the flask causes a series of physical transformations—a cycle of color changes—that are the stimuli for transformative psychic meditations. First, the burnt material darkens, a blackness symbolized by the raven in illustrations, a blackness that represents an opening phase of withdrawal into darkness. Ancient alchemist texts noted cultural fears of the darkness but claimed that those with the courage to look would be rewarded by the discovery of new depths and vistas. Next, the material whitens, represented by the swan. There is a vacillation between floating on the surface and a dipping into the mud below, finding spiritual purity in unpromising primal material. White is considered the stage of catharsis that glimpses new possibilities. Then, a rush of colors and iridescence, the peacock's tail, is sometimes mistaken for the end of the work, but this prematurity must await further transformations. Next, when the hydrochloric acid of salt is mixed with nitric acid, there forms an aqua regia, a green-tinged fluid, the Green Lion, that is the tie to nature. A second whitening, the Queen, the feminine, and reddening, the masculine, the Red King, have been the basis for emphasizing the sexual aspects of gender dualities, illustrated in the sixteenth-century text *Rosarium Philosophorum*, by a male-female coupling and subsequently misunderstood by some misguided alchemists or worse, who sought a shortcut to magic through sex acts. Finally, we are left with the residue that symbolizes the Phoenix, the personality reborn out of the crucible of transformation, the Philosopher's Stone created out of the ground of inner experience, out of the dualistic energies of the soul forces, by which we seek the full potentiality of being human.

I was convinced, but it was a setup. Bluestone told us that alchemists have been forced to adapt to such a rapid evolution of advanced molecular and pharmacological principles, and were in such undersupply, that they could no longer afford the time-intensive attention to inner experience.

They should now be considered "chemists," he said, with communication skills.

When we arrived at the colony, it was already dusk. Bluestone, now Bradford, his beard unbraided, took us directly to the field where the prayer service began in concert with the simplicity of the gospels. Beneath the plush canopy of emerging stars we listened, and waited for direction, for a sign, for our heavenly fruit.

BPSI 2004
RESILIENCY: JELLYFISH

We had site visitors this year. We had site visitors from the American Psychoanalytic Association. The American Psychoanalytic Association sent the most site visitors that they had ever sent anywhere. They were at meetings. They were at seminars. They were in my house. At the institute we served a lot of food. Diana allowed us to eat upstairs. After several days the site visitors told us that we were great. Top drawer. The best they had seen. We told the site visitors that we liked them, too. The candidates told the site visitors that their report did not address an important problem facing the institute—that psychoanalysis is about to disappear—so we talked about that too.

Piotr Naskrecki, the evolutionary biologist presently at Harvard, was in the news this year. Piotr Naskrecki was in the news protesting our indifference to the extinction of species of invertebrates. He said that *spineless* animals are underrepresented on the endangered species list.

The site visitors noted that we meet in large bodies and talk a lot but don't do anything. They suggested that we meet in a small group so that we can make decisions. So we met in a small group and decided on ways to eliminate exclusion.

The site visitors said that one day the father had all the girls and all the power and so we killed him and ate him and now we prevent anyone from assuming any authority or making any judgments out of deferred obedience based in guilt. They said we are like babies with notochords.

I injured my spine this year. I followed a leader into a glade. He had been a ski instructor for twenty-five years on the same mountain. He had been a Green Beret. He had seen action in three military conflicts.

He got us lost in a patch of trees the size of a small yard. I fell over on a tree. Paramedics took an hour to dig me out. I yelled a lot. They put a devise around my head that looked like the kapfthalter that the father Schreber put on the son Schreber to improve his posture. They put a kapfthalter on my head, but the problem was in my lower back. They said that they knew but they had a protocol. They took me on a sled into an ambulance and filled me with intravenous morphine like I was at war—at war in ski boots.

More than ninety percent of living animals lack a backbone. The diversity of the spineless is so great—ranging from protozoa to the giant squid—that the taxonomic term, the subphylum name, "Invertebrata," is no longer valid in modern classifications. Vertebrata remains valid.

The orthopedic surgeons said that they would not need to operate and gave me a lot of medications that made me sick. They made me sick and caused me to lose many important fluids and I had to go back into the hospital to get them back. My brother-in-law, an internist who specializes in pain management, said that I should go to a physiATrist.

In 1938, Frank Krusner at the Mayo Clinic coined the term "physiATry" to describe physicians who add physical agents—heat, water, electricity, and such agents as dated from the time of Hippocrates—to medical therapeutics for the treatment of musculoskeletal and neurological disorders. In 1946, the American Medical Association Council on Physical Medicine voted to sponsor the term physiATry, with the emphasis on the third syllable. PhysiATrists are very sensitive about the correct pronunciation of their specialty. Their texts and letterheads inevitably reproduce a graphic representation of the stressed third syllable in large block phonetic symbols. The pronunciation appears as such in most American dictionaries and throughout the English-speaking world except on the East Coast, where we say "phySIatrist" because—we don't care. We think "physiATrist" sounds silly.

The site visitors said that the absence of a backbone need not impede our efforts to hold onto our building and to achieve suchadaptations and outreach as to secure our survival. They suggested that we consider the example of the coelenterates, planktonic marine members constructed around a central body cavity, the coelenteron, in short, jellyfish, that have survived the oceans for over six million years, survived extremes of temperature, salination, and the very sliming of their reefs such that, today, when toxins have killed the reef algae and thereby starved the small fish and caused the large fish, in turn, to disappear, indigenous fishermen have been forced to turn to jellyfish for food. They cook them. They taste crunchy.

Specifically, the site visitors drew our attention—for learning, for inspiration—to the adaptations and outreach of the *Physalia*, the Portuguese man-of-war. The *Physalia* represents a noble experiment of nonhierarchical cooperation among attached multicellular organisms. It is a team, a floating colony. In this happy division of labor, some individuals swim, some sting, and some float, and together they achieve an extraordinary level of complexity on a colonial plan. Marine biologists refer to the *Physalia* as a *superorganism*. In evolution, it is a dead end. The tip of a branch. Life proceeds through the flatworms. Regardless, the purple-hued, gas-filled, bladder-like float waves a crest of adaptation that acts like a sail and takes the superorganism whichever way the winds blow. Polyps beneath the float sprout tentacles that can stretch fifty meters in order to reach out and touch the client organisms in whom they find an interest. Small fish that live among the tentacles, the

Nomeus gronovii, are partially immune to the toxin-releasing nemato-cysts. Sometimes the fish eat the tentacles, which regenerate, and some-times the tentacles eat the fish, which do not.

The physiatrists told me that they would have to look at my scans themselves because they could see fractures of the bone that other spe-cialists, the orthopedic surgeons and the radiologists, could not see. They said that the orthopedic surgeons saw only things that called for operations. They said that the radiologists did not see the fractures because they looked at *too many* films. They told me they saw a fracture on my film, and then they took more films and told me they saw three fractures on my films. Fractures that no one else had seen.

Physiatrists and psychoanalysts have areas of coincident history and concerns. Both formed professional organizations in the last century. Both treat long-term, frequently subjective complaints with modalities that resist empirical validation in the individual case. Both rely on a relationship with the treater. Both have a scientistic pole seeking inclu-sion in organized medicine. Both have a more intangible pole that veers into alternative modes.

The United Kingdom site for physiatry, for example, shares space with the writings and visual art of Jonathan Earl Bowser. Mr. Bowser's representations of mythic naturalism, he explains, present dreamscapes of the First Ancestors, the omnimorphic parents from which all forms derive, ever dying and ever reborn. The ventral surfaces of his mythic goddesses emphasize erotic protuberances, but the paintings are struc-tured around the stippled line of spinous processes that mark the dorsum. My physiatrist said that he was not familiar with Mr. Bowser's work.

Whereas psychoanalysis is born of hysterical conversions and the traumas of war, physiatry derives from war injuries and polio. In recent years, physiatrists have multiplied and grown young in response to the needs of the aged. Psychoanalysts, in turn, have aged. Newell Fischer, our president, wrote that he asked a Young Mathematician to study our age demographics. The Young Mathematician determined that by this time next year the average member of the American Psychoanalytic Association will be eligible for Social Security. The average training analyst will be older still. It seems plausible to expect, however, that in the near future, with a death rate exceeding our birth rate, our average age will be much younger but we will be extinct. The site visitors said that they were not familiar with the Young Mathematician.

The site visitors concluded their report by referring to a Boston institution facing crises that mirror our own. Only a few years ago, the New England Aquarium was flush. They completed an IMAX theater and there were plans for a $125 million expansion of their central cavity. Last year, however, they lost $20 million, laid off over twenty employees, became the first major institution to lose accreditation from the AZA (the Association of Zoos and Aquariums), and struggled for funds to fix their roof.

And yet, they remain afloat. They are back this year with a new exhibition, their spirits more crested than benthic. The exhibition, titled "Jellies," features the ever buoyant members of the phylum Coelenterata. Reviewers have been enthusiastic. They say the exhibit is great. Top drawer. The best they have seen.

BPSI 2005
OPENNESS: THE BUILDING

I was advised to speak about the proposal to sell our building at 15 Commonwealth Avenue.

My understanding is that our leaders called a meeting to recommend that we sell the building. They said we should be transparent and inclusive, and they said we should not be paralyzed.

Some people said we should not sell the building because we do not know what will happen and we might become unhappy.

Our transparent leaders offered a survey that asked if we would support selling the building if we knew ahead of time that we would be happy.

A supermajority—more than half, less than two-thirds—of those who responded said they would support being happy.

A superminority—more than one-third and less than one-half—said they would support being unhappy if certain specified others would be unhappy too.

Our transparent leaders understood the result to represent a mandate to flush ourselves, to flush ourselves with funds, if we can secure a new building with better parking and a room for socials.

We also had the opportunity to participate in an active online discussion that enabled psychoanalysts of all levels of seniority, and psychoanalysts representing many different theoretical perspectives, to offer their views of the real estate market.

In what was assumed to be a misprint, Tsol Yenom posted, "Be it ever so Hubble, there's no place like Home."

It appears likely that the Hubble space telescope will be decommissioned in 2007. Louis Lanzerotti, chair of the National Research

Council, defended a shuttle rescue mission to replace Hubble's failing batteries, but Sean O'Keefe at NASA said preserving Hubble was too expensive given the state of NASA finances. There was a hue and a cry. On the hill, Congressman Sherwood Boehlert (R-NY), chair of the House Science Committee, said that he was sympathetic to Hubble but that we should not be emotional. Congressman Ken Calvert, chair of the Space Aeronautics Subcommittee, praised Hubble. He said that Hubble had enabled us to glimpse black holes, to watch comets slam into Jupiter, to watch stars born and to watch stars die. He said that we had learned more from Hubble in a decade than in the four hundred years of astronomy since Galileo. Then he excused himself to attend to other business.

The NASA administrator reversed himself and endorsed a robot servicing mission. The 2006 fiscal budget, however, did not contain funding for a robot servicing mission. A new NASA administrator has emphasized funding for the international space station, which offers better docking and is more inclusive but doesn't see anything. Because of its size and shape, Hubble has been compared to an orbiting school bus. A future robot mission will attach a propulsion module to de-orbit the school bus and park it in the Pacific Ocean.

We have reason to suspect the presence of Dark Forces.

Freud argued that the distortions and self-deceptions that hamper our efforts to see ourselves and our world are as difficult for us to see as the air that we breathe. He searched for a new method that would provide more reliable psychological data than could be arrived at through solitary introspection. Shortly after Freud's death, astronomer Lyman Spitzer argued that our efforts to see the universe and our place in it are hampered by the distorting effects of the air we breathe. Spitzer proposed a space-based observatory that would provide more reliable astronomical data than could be arrived at through terrestrial telescopes. When his dream was realized and the first space telescope was launched into orbit, one of the first discoveries was a confirmation of Dark Forces.

The usual knock on online discussions is that they tend to be dominated by a few enthusiastic malcontents with too much time on their hands.

Tony Melos posted his concern that the introduction of suspicions about Dark Forces into our discussions was misguided—that our push-pull dualistic theories incline us to Manichean speculations about the balance of light and dark in our world, that astronomic Dark Forces have little to do with questions of good and evil, even less to do with questions of motive, and more to do, first, with the Dark Energy that Einstein conjectured balanced gravity and thereby avoided the collapse of the universe imagined as the Big Crunch, and, second, with the Dark Matter that put the brakes on universal expansion that might otherwise lead to the Big Rip. His reassurance did not address the more troubling Hubble-based observation, however, that the Dark Forces previously assumed to be concentrated at the margins of the universe are now recognized to be concentrated in the immediate vicinity.

Guy Pinterra posted his neuroscientific speculations that those who cling to the building do so with their reptilian brains. He based his conclusion on a report that he saw on the *Lehrer News Hour* in which NIH neuroscientists explained that successful stock market investment strategies privilege the prefrontal cortex over the reptilian brain. They said that when we cling to the past rather than adapt to the future we are acting like reptiles. They had brain scans and a rubber model of the brain to support their claims.

Guy Pinterra was once instrumental in the care of our turtle, Jerry, when torpor complicated his treatment for shell rot. I told Guy that Jerry passed this year and was buried with his building. He said that Jerry was a reptile and had no choice.

Mandel Fogel posted that he chooses austerity over ornate temples. He has modeled his path on the way of the Mahavihara. Twelfth-century Khmers followed the missionaries of the Mahavihara into rebellion against their *deva-rajas*, their god-kings. They abandoned the great temples of Angkor to the jungle, they leveled social hierarchies, and they divested themselves of their specialness. While it is true that the immediate consequence of their decision was centuries of subjugation to the more hierarchically organized T'ais, and stagnation and strife from which they have yet to emerge, it seems likely, Mandel says, that an architectural solution will, at some point, suggest itself.

Tsol Yenom posted a Chinese proverb from *Sandcastles*, his work on architectural abandonment: "The peasant walks on the house of the Emperor." He followed with a whirlwind tour of building-loss. The Sumerians raised mud settlements into terraced multistoried temple towers—the book of Genesis says, "They had bricks for stone, and slime they had for mortar." Their towers inspired the story of Babel. Where are their ruins today? The Greek temples at Acragas, monuments of Doric simplicity, were built by men of whom it was said, "They dine as if they expected to die tomorrow, and build as if they expected to live forever." Now the temples lie in empty fields. The cost of the great public works of Egypt and Rome consumed the empires that created them. And, a thousand years ago, the Indian Temples of Love at Kajuraho were built deep in the forest by thousands of architects, sculptors, and masons. Today they are overgrown with bushes and weeds, lost to all except the tourists who seek out their famously graph-ic representations of tantric love.

Our leaders call for calm. They tell us that they sat down with great wealth and they offer the excitement of doing so as hope to the next generation. They say that the universe will still be here even while we wait to launch the next space telescope a few years from now. They believe that the trainees who are temporarily stranded, blind, and homeless, in the interim, will be okay. They encourage a return to a more analytic perspective. They tell us that when the next space tele-scope is launched it will peel back the galaxies in the deep field revealed by Hubble, it will bring us closer to the primal scene, the conception, than we have ever been before, closer to the post-Bang, first three hun-dred thousand years known only as the Dark Zone. If Hubble saw the distant, departing child galaxies of our universal origin, the James Webb space telescope will reach into infancy; it will expose the full arc of time, from the primordial seeds to the controlled descent; and it will, at long last, put our parking issues in their proper perspective.

BPSI 2006
OPTIMISM: MIRACLE MIKE

Can we be positive? Can we be optimistic and resilient?

There are reasons to be optimistic, for example, about quicksand.

The terrifying screams of secondary characters sucked to their horrifying ends are so much Hollywood myth, according to researchers at the University of Amsterdam. In fact, the fearsome soup is a sandy mixture that, at two grams per cubic centimeter, is twice the density of the human body. As such, all we need to do is remain calm and still and we will rise and float more easily than we would on water. But if we panic and flail, the liquefied sand will separate and form sandy slurry so dense and impenetrable that we will sink as if encased in stone.

It is a time for resilience. Earlier this academic year, at my eighty-ninth hour of BPSI administrative meetings, so noted in my date book, it came to me that our singular, concentrated, unwavering focus on the criteria for selection of Training and Supervising Psychoanalysts—a focus maintained in the setting of problems in the profession so deep and diverse as to threaten the field and cut to the very marrow of our professional identities—represents a form of prayer. These meetings were not about external realities. The content of the meetings was merely the day residue for the dream of the meeting, a dream to be apprehended through private reverie. At that moment I realized that my own resonant waking dream image of a central bolt being placed against my skull—the central bolt is a rod used in slaughterhouses to penetrate and destroy brain tissue prior to death by exsanguination—must have to do with the controversy generated by the refusal of the arbiters of the kashrut and halal dietary laws to permit the use of the central bolt prior to slaughter. The point is this: Briefly this winter, in the midst of our crisis, our attention wavered and there were two months during which TA selection was only discussed and was not the lead agenda item. An understandable crisis of faith. By the spring, however, it was back in full flower as our exclusive focus in every setting. Such is resilience and the capacity to stay the course.

It is a time to keep our heads, but there are reasons to be optimistic about the alternative. On September 10, 1945, Lloyd and Clara Olsen used an ax to slaughter their 5 1/2-month-old Wyandotte rooster, soon to be known as Miracle Mike. After losing his head, Mike continued to stand, strut, and balance on the highest perches as if nothing had happened. The Olsens decided to feed him ground grain and water through his severed esophagus. They added bits of gravel for his gizzard and sucked out his mucus with a syringe to prevent him from choking. Hope Wade, a promoter, made him a star. Mike toured the western states for eighteen months and appeared in *Life* magazine. (They brought along his head in a jar, until their cat ate the head, and then they substituted another rooster's head. In the jar.) The Olsens made a lot of money. Many others attempted to replicate their feat. One rooster, Lucky, lived eleven days. In March of 1947, Miracle Mike choked to death in a Phoenix motel room because Lloyd forgot the syringe at the sideshow. The date of the death can only be estimated because Lloyd covered up his error. He said that he had sold Mike. For years afterward, stories appeared in the press that claimed that Mike remained on tour.

It is a time for resilience. Some feared that our recent troubles might slow our efforts to systematically eliminate evaluative judgments from all aspects of instruction, progression, and selection. However, our aspirations to remove vetting of TA applicants and the imminent demise of national certification will proudly burst the final two buttons and complete our transformation from a shrinking profession into a really big study group.

It is a time for keeping our bearings, but there are reasons to be optimistic about being at sea. Of the 10^{10} earth-like planets predicted by statistical modeling to reside in our galaxy, it now appears that a large number are complete water worlds with no appreciable landmass. Sean Raymond of the University of Washington in Seattle looked at the statistics of planet formation in forty-two different scenarios based upon our own solar system. They simulated planetary embryos inside a Jupiter-like giant. The embryos gathered smaller bodies of rock and ice called planetesimals and produced one to four earth-sized planets per giant, over half of which were water planets. In our galaxy, having no place to stand is the norm.

It is a time for resilience. Some feared the proponents of the sale of our building would suffer the painful hangover of a hypomanic libidinization of money and charismatic leadership. But. They are back with new proposals for even larger real estate transactions and bushels of sodden cash to keep us buoyant, unless the flailing sinks us like a stone.

It is a time to be adaptive but there are reasons to be optimistic about obsolescence. How often have we psychoanalysts been compared to manufacturers of buggy whips? And yet. "Whip City," Westfield, Massachusetts, once the hub of buggy whip production, employing 95 percent of the 1890s workforce to that end, is showing signs of life. After the bankruptcies of the 1940s, only two companies remained. One chased a more lucrative market in braided fish line, but one company, Westfield Whip Company, held on. They are prospering. They make custom whips for a variety of applications. Some go to the traditional livestock industry. Some go to discreet sex supply shops advertising on the Internet. Some go to aging baby boomers who, now too old to ride horses, have fueled a resurgent interest in carriage driving.

The 150th anniversary of Freud's birth was observed in major psychoanalytic centers throughout the country. BPSI, the largest, did not directly acknowledge the occasion although we did schedule three special meetings that month on the issue of the selection criteria for Training and Supervising Psychoanalysts. Freud liked to celebrate his birthday by articulating morbid assessments and prognostications of his own demise. From an early age he described himself as freezing, becoming inorganic, ready to die, and losing penetrating force. And yet. While he never had to deal with loss of market share, he did manage to muddle on, producing volume after volume of creative genius through fifty years of illness, child loss, dislocation, war, and genocide. At the heart of Freudian pessimism is evidence of the other, and of extraordinary resilience. We don't talk much about psychoanalytic eschatology, about our theory of Last Things, but there are reasons to be optimistic about what may grow from the End of Days.

Well, we should not squabble.

In Alfred Hitchcock's film *Lifeboat*, the people on the boat start fighting, and one of them says squabbling will just "make the ocean bigger and the boat smaller."

Fifty years from now, those planning to attend the celebration of the 200th birthday may find some of our current dilemmas less pressing.

The more optimistic futurists anticipate that the Singularity will have arrived—that moment when our computational capacity exceeds that of the human brain—and, with it, a quantum leap in progress that will, at long last, reverse Freudian skepticism about the thin skein of civilization overlaying depths of savagery. Rather, they anticipate a large rider on a little horse, and the animal nature that has been the source of such mischief will be an object of nostalgia. The more pessimistic predictions place much of the eastern seaboard underwater.

If we are dry, I imagine we will manage a party. And if we are wet, I expect that our good ideas will rise and float again. If we can stay calm.

ABOUT THE AUTHOR

Dr. Phillip Freeman is a psychiatrist and a Training and Supervising Psychoanalyst at the Boston Psychoanalytic Institute. He has faculty appointments at Harvard Medical School and at the Boston University Medical School where he was director of Medical Student Education and a vice chair in the Department of Psychiatry. His publications include writing about psychoanalytic education, psychopathology, and applied psychoanalysis. He discusses and consults to productions of films and plays in the Boston area. His private practice is in Newton, Massachusetts.